Autism and the Extended Family

A Guide for Those Outside the Immediate Family
Who Know and Love Someone with Autism

Raun Melmed, M.D.
and Maria Wheeler, M.Ed.

Autism and the Extended Family: A Guide for Those Outside the Immediate Family Who Know and Love Someone with Autism

All marketing and publishing rights guaranteed to and reserved by

FUTURE HORIZONS

817-277-0727
817-277-2270 (fax)
E-mail: info@FHautism.com
www.FHautism.com

ISBN: 9781935274667

Table of Contents

Foreword by Eustacia Cutler

I n Chapter 11 of this splendid new family guide to autism, Dr. Raun Melmed and Maria Wheeler allude to the much loved story of the plane that was meant to take us to Italy, but instead lands us in Holland.

For most of us, Holland is not where the plane lands. Holland is an easy country filled with friendly people who respond sensibly to newcomers.

No, the plane we're on takes us spiraling down the *Alice in Wonderland* Rabbit Hole into an unpredictable world alive with noisy behavior that demands our total attention, only to change as fast as we've figured it out.

Where have we landed and who is this small screaming creature who shudders at our slightest touch and won't look at us?

Up until now, we thought all babies liked us and wanted to be with us. We used to say, "A baby needs a mother to know she's a baby and a mother needs a baby to know she's a mother." Not anymore!

Okay, then what about Dad? Dad likes to fix things, but his baby's behavior can't be "fixed" not in the old familiar father-to-son way. When a man can't handle his own son, what kind of a man is he?

"Few conditions are as puzzling and mysterious as autism," Melmed and Wheeler write.

Indeed yes, welcome to the Rabbit Hole World where autism scrambles all our old notions about raising children.

Autism takes over and almost at once it's hard for parents to hang onto who it is we thought we were. Along with the daily tasks of caretaking, which can be formidable, our individual sense of self gets shaky. And with it, how we think we're perceived by others.

At this point, we also find we're struggling to hang onto old customs and shared neighborhood values in a rapidly evolving culture that puts a higher value on personal identity and individual achievement.

In truth, the old customs and values are pretty much outmoded for everyone. And in their places, we have an Internet gadget that lures us into a virtual world of instant answers. All it takes is a finger sweeping gesture on the shiny face of a new cell phone.

Going to Australia? Dr. Google tells us what shots to get. Took the wrong turn to Minneola? GPS straightens us out. Need a new life partner? Virtual dating sites have the perfect mate.

Welcome to the world of easy answers — only there are no easy answers for autism. But if you are looking for a moment of much needed peace of mind, here's a wireless head phone. Wear it and you're isolated — dancing alone to disc jockey music only you can hear.

In this shifting, fragmented confusion where everyone and everything is up for grabs, how are Autism Spectrum Disorders (ASD) parents to manage?

First lesson of Rabbit Hole World is nobody can raise an autism spectrum child alone. Each family needs step-by-step professional guidance. And each family also needs an **extended family** to circle the wagons around them.

Sounds good, but how do we know "professional guidance" isn't just one more Google answer? And who will help us assemble an extended family?

Now's the moment to turn to the book written by Raun Melmed, a pediatrician who understands and specializes in guiding families through the Rabbit Hole maze of neurological challenge, lost identity, and social screw-up.

Along with extensive pediatric know-how and some 30 years of hands-on practice here in the states, Dr. Melmed offers advice grounded in his own upbringing in South Africa, a beautiful country, scarred by generations of apartheid "separateness."

In the years when Cape Town was suffering under apartheid, Raun, the child must have grown to manhood secure in the protective warmth of an extended family. This carefully thought-out guide book conjures up the old phrase "kith and kin." "Kith" is a forgotten word for friends and neighbors, coined when fathers and sons, cousins and in-laws lived and worked together in close relationships on farms, in stores, and at institutions of learning. Kith and kin must have been crucial to Melmed's boyhood, not just for extended family comfort, but for safety as well.

In his own words:

"Growing up in South Africa made me acutely aware of the differences among people during a time when apartheid attempted to divide them from one another. I resolved to work toward celebrating those differences and focusing on those with developmental challenges."

To this declaration, Dr. Melmed adds a colorful sidebar:

"It I weren't a doctor, I would be an actor. The unfolding human drama parading through my office on a day-to-day basis is what nourishes me — being privy to the joys and tears of the families and their children. So if not in real life, I would choose the stage."

Dr. Melmed's words sent me searching for those of Athol Fugard, renowned actor/playwright who also grew up in Cape Town.

"In the theatre, of course," writes Fugard, "my fascination lies with the 'living moment' — the actual, the real, the immediate, there before my eyes, even it if shares in the transient fate of all living moments. I suppose the theatre uses more of the actual substance of life than any other art ... flesh and blood, sweat, the human voice, real pain, real times."

Despite two lives based on different professions, both men know firsthand what it's like to suffer one another man's contempt, if not savage hate.

They also share a deeply felt drive to remedy and refocus the damage that acts of deliberate isolation — whether oppression in South Africa,

bullying in an American school yard, or subtle shunning by neighbors —
do to both victim and perpetrator.

In *Autism and the Extended Family*, Dr. Melmed and Maria Wheeler
lay out guiding steps for a family's possible transformation. "When we can
do that and accept that loved one who is ours, we will be healed."

The word "heal" means "whole." No longer fragmented.

No longer dancing in lonely isolation.

CHAPTER 1

Introduction

D oes someone you love have autism? With the dramatic increase in the number of individuals diagnosed with autism, you very likely do. When a child is diagnosed with autism the entire family is impacted, along with extended family members and friends.

Sometimes we may feel helpless or frustrated in these situations, especially when we are very close to the child and his or her parents. Few conditions are as puzzling and mysterious as autism, which can make us feel unsure and even powerless. We might not know what to say, what to do, or how to help. Extended family members have a very important role to play, and the goal of this book is to help understand how valuable all family members are and to provide practical suggestions on how to help.

1

So what is an extended family?

For the purpose of this book, we consider "extended family" to include any-one who is connected to the child or adult impacted by autism, either as a relative, partner, or close friend.

Who would you consider to be a member of your own extended family? Of course there is the *nuclear* family. Those are the people that live togeth-er in one house. Traditionally, we have thought of them as parents and chil-dren. Increasingly, however, step-parents, half-siblings, step-siblings, and other adults have become involved. A better term might be the "blended family." There might be adoptive children living in the family or even foster children living under the same roof. A parent might be married, single, gay, or even LAT!—living apart together.

By extended family, we usually refer to families who may be, but are usually not, living together. These families include grandparents, aunts, uncles, cousins, nephews, and nieces. And, of course, there are the in-laws, parents-in-law, and brothers and sisters-in-law. Today the term is common-ly used for family members whether or not they live together within the same household.

Extended families may often live under the same roof. This set-up can in-clude multiple generations in the family. A common scenario is one in which a grandparent, adult children, and often grandchildren all live together for financial or care-giving reasons. Nationwide, more than 2.5 million grand-parents have taken on the primary responsibility of raising grandchildren in what AARP calls "grandfamilies". Oftentimes, a grandchild has autism.

In today's world, families are often scattered across the country. Grand-parents, aunts, and uncles might live far away. That is just one of the rea-sons we form close bonds with friends who may be filling the roles of blood relatives. These friends are an enormous source of love and support to all of us, especially for families affected by autism. They rightly fill the role of family and are included and welcomed into the extended family!

There are clear advantages to having a large extended family. Securi-ty and sharing resources during a crisis seem the most obvious of these. Members of the extended family can also be role models to help perpetuate desired behavior and cultural values. They form a supportive network that adds to the fun at family gatherings, birthday celebrations, and so on.

Understandably, it is harder to attend social events and participate in them when a child has autism. This gives us even more reason to provide the most effective support system for our child and his or her family. Sometimes parents tell us they have given up hope for successful play dates for their children with autism. "What's the point?" they ask. "It never works out. The kid comes over and mine just sits in the corner and does not share or participate in any way."

Sometimes parents may decide, consciously or unconsciously, to avoid events because of their child's behavior or because they feel unwelcome. This can result in isolation, which is clearly not in anyone's best interest.

Those are precisely the types of situations in which we need to encourage and support opportunities for social interactions when extra play dates need to be set up, rather than avoiding play dates. Of course, these play dates may not be like typical play dates, and may need to be structured using appropriate interventions. Of course, that takes expertise and work, but it's what is needed and it will help your child learn how to have a successful play date.

Positive outcomes for children with autism and their families can be achieved if extended family members learn, understand, and participate more in the child's life; such interaction will enable the family circle to experience the joy of successfully participating in the growth and learning of a beautiful child. Everyone benefits.

Working together as an extended family for the benefit of a child with autism takes effort. It will likely present a challenge for each family member to look beyond themselves, past any previous opinions or roles adopted prior to working together to support the child with autism. All extended family members must be aware of their own strengths and weaknesses, along with any past events that may present challenges to working together for a common cause. Such challenges are typical and should be expected and resolved supportively. This will be a journey like no other. Most people in a family want to help, get along, and be together. It's time to begin taking the first steps toward setting aside our differences and working together to help our loved one with autism grow, learn, and thrive. Be brave and work through any conflicts, even in the face of drama or hostility that may arise when family members feel so passionately about what the child needs. The first priority is always the child and his or her immediate family.

Are you a good extended family member?

Most extended families are wonderfully accepting of children with autism and their parents. The family and child can only benefit from your support as an extended family member! When the extended family is supportive and helpful, the child and its immediate family are encouraged to be involved in activities as much as is practical and tolerable. Extended families can provide a wonderful support system for the immediate family of a child with autism.

Do some extended family members have difficulty accepting a child's diagnosis of autism, the symptoms, and/or the treatment program? Do they understand and honor what the child can tolerate or do they try to impose their own will and structure on the child or on the parent? It is by example and through education that extended family members can learn to positively impact a child with autism, beyond what comes naturally. Education is a powerful coping tool. Learning as much as you can about autism is critical to being an effective source of change, growth, and support.

We all need extended families; loved ones who can act as extra cheerleaders and a built-in support group. That is the reason for this book. They say it takes a village to raise a child. At the very least, a child with autism needs a team, and every member of the extended family team is impacted by autism. Autism is definitely a family affair.

Please refer to **Activity A** in the Activity section to understand who may be part of your extended family.

CHAPTER 2

Welcome to the World of Autism!

The world of autism is often confusing and overwhelming for everyone! Parents, the person who has autism, siblings, and extended family members all have many unanswered questions.

Autistic Spectrum Disorder (ASD) is a neurodevelopmental disorder that continues throughout a person's life. It used to be called Pervasive Developmental Disorder and included Autistic Disorder, Asperger's Disorder (also known as Asperger's syndrome) and PDD-NOS, but it is now called ASD. We use the term "autism" or ASD in this book.

Your loved one was diagnosed with an autism spectrum disorder because he demonstrates significant difficulties:

- Communicating effectively using words, facial expressions, body language, tone of voice, and eye gaze as part of a cooperative, reciprocal exchange with other people;
- Understanding and responding to what other people are trying to communicate through words, facial expressions, tone of voice, body language, and eye gaze;
- Understanding and using social skills, including playing and interacting with others, using cooperative give-and-take gestures, and expressing feelings in an acceptable manner; and
- Repetitive, rigid, and/or restrictive patterns of behavior, reasoning, or thinking.

 CASE EXAMPLE

Lisa is 12 years old. She was recently diagnosed with Asperger's syndrome, which is a type of ASD. Lisa is very smart. She can talk for hours about her favorite topic, but walks away if someone asks her a question about something that does not interest her. Lisa also yells and throws tantrums. Many people think she is rude and "spoiled." They do not realize her behavior is directly related to having autism. Lisa has started Applied Behavioral Analysis (ABA) therapy and is learning what to do and say when other people ask her a question, no matter what the topic is. She is also learning acceptable ways to talk and act when she is frustrated or upset.

When we say autism is a neurodevelopmental condition, it means autism is an illness of the nervous system caused by genetic, metabolic, or other biological factors. Parents do not cause autism. Autism develops independently of what parents and caretakers do as a child is growing and learning. Everyone who has autism is an individual person. No two people with autism are the same. Although every person with autism has difficulties with communication, social functioning, and rigid, repetitive or restrictive patterns of thinking or behaving, each individual is affected by these difficulties in unique ways.

The most effective treatments for autism are based on behavioral principles, sometimes called Applied Behavioral Analysis (ABA), and include Pivotal Response Training (PRT). Other treatments include Treatment and Education of Autistic and Related Communication Handicapped Children (TEACCH), Floor time, and Picture Exchange Communication System (PECS). Educational opportunities within the public school system are available to all children and include potential access to speech therapy and occupational therapy (OT). Medical treatments can be used to address behavioral, sleep-related, and other physical challenges. There is no known cure for autism, but with treatment, any individual's outcome can be optimized.

 CAUTION

Avoid assuming your loved one's immediate family is the only one affected by autism. Autism in your family will affect everyone whose lives are connected to your family. Help one another learn about autism and how everyone can work together to support your loved one's growth, learning, well-being, and happiness—each in their own way.

At the same time, it is important to recognize that many people's lives may be impacted by the special needs of a loved one who has autism. The effects of autism are far reaching and often affect your loved one's relationships with other people who do not live in the family home. This includes relatives, step-family, family friends, partners and children of relatives and family friends, and relatives and friends living in other towns, states, or countries.

 CAUTION

Avoid blaming parents or assuming that poor discipline is the reason a child with autism has "meltdowns" or acts in ways that seem rude or self-ish. Many children with autism need to be directly and repeatedly taught what to do and say in social situations. Learning simple social skills that other people readily learn may take months or years for a person with autism to learn. Your loved ones need caring support and understanding when learning how to cope with these issues.

 CASE EXAMPLE

Manny does not talk. In the past, he grabbed food and drinks from other people, climbed up on counters and took food out of the cupboards. He opened the refrigerator and took food. Manny had tantrums when he could not find what he was searching for. His mother tried to help, but she sometimes could not guess what he wanted and Manny would scream, cry, and hit her. Manny went to therapy and learned how to give people a picture to ask for what he wanted. He is starting to say a few words and has had very few meltdowns since learning a better way to communicate.

The effects of autism are relentless; they occur day after day, week after week, month after month, and year after year. The strain is often overwhelming and affects physical, emotional, and financial wellbeing. Understanding these far-reaching influences can help you support your loved ones whose lives have been touched by autism.

It is also important to recognize how other people's lives are affected by autism, even if their lives are not impacted on a daily basis.

Friends, relatives, and co-workers may have difficulty understanding why the parent of a child who has autism:

- does not attend social functions;
- naps during the day;
- cancels plans at the last minute;
- cannot find a babysitter;
- is in deep debt, has no extra money, or cannot afford the basics;
- frequently goes to, or talks about medical or therapy appointments;
- does not attend family or work-related gatherings;
- "won't discipline" his/her child.

Learn more about autism so you can understand why a parent might display some or all of these behaviors. You may be surprised to learn that your loved one wants to socialize with you, but cannot find a babysitter who is trained to care for her child safely. Your employee may be late sometimes because his child has overwhelming panic attacks if he sees a dark cloud while walking to the car. Your co-worker may want to attend social gatherings after work, but must go home so his spouse can sleep before she has to stay up all night with a child who does not sleep. Your cousin may not attend the family reunion because his child cannot tolerate large groups of people and he doesn't want to disrupt the event for others. Your daughter may not appear to be disciplining her child because she understands that her child's behavior is due to being overwhelmed by over-stimulation, so the best strategy is to calmly help her child access a less stimulating environment.

Together we can learn how autism affects our loved ones and how we can better support one another. An important step in providing such support is learning how to effectively understand, prevent, and respond to the behaviors of our family members who have autism so they can function more successfully in the extended family network. It is also important to recognize that support can be provided directly or indirectly. Some family members may not be comfortable providing direct support in the form of interacting with the person who has autism, but may still want to help. They can still provide great support by indirectly helping.

 CASE EXAMPLE

An uncle steps up!

Terrell did not have much patience with his nephew, Ben, who had autism. Ben did not talk and seemed to avoid him. Ben preferred to be outdoors most of the time. Terrell was very good at repairing and building. He noticed a section of the fence outside Ben's house was leaning and offered to repair it. Ben's parents had been worried that the fence would fall down and Ben might run off, but they were so overwhelmed just getting through each day, that they had not fixed the fence. They greatly appreciated Terrell's help. Terrell was happy to find a way to help them. He realized how challenging each day was for Ben's parents. When he came to visit he would look for any repairs that were needed and would take care of them.

CASE EXAMPLES

A sister's support

Jaz wanted to help her sister with her son, Beau, who had autism, but was afraid of Beau's violent outbursts. Her sister was a single mom and could not even cook dinner without numerous interruptions from Beau's outbursts and demands. Jaz offered to cook dinner for her sister and Beau three evenings a week. She always made enough so there were leftovers for her sister to reheat the other weekday evenings. Jaz also became more familiar with Beau's behavior patterns when she was at the house cooking. She learned how to predict and prevent many of his outbursts, which helped her feel more comfortable with him. Over time they established a closer relationship. Jaz's sister greatly appreciated the support.

A granny pitches in

Eva's mother knew date nights had been important to Eva and her husband before they had their daughter, Luna. She was no longer comfortable babysitting for Luna, who had autism, but Eva's parents could not afford a babysitter. Eva's mother hired a babysitter one night each month so they could continue having date nights.

CHAPTER 3

How Lives Are Affected after Autism is Diagnosed

Grief following a diagnosis of Autism

We often recognize that someone experiences grief when a loved one passes away. However, grief also occurs when someone experiences a significant loss. Several stages of emotional reaction can follow such loss. When parents hear their child has autism, they experience grief due to the loss of the child they envisioned or expected; the loss of the child they dreamed would learn, grow, thrive, and succeed without significant challenges. When extended family members learn that their loved one has autism, they grieve as well. Grandparents grieve over the loss of the grandchild they envisioned. Step-parents grieve over the loss of the stepchild they anticipated watching and/or helping grow up. Close family friends and other relatives also grieve over the loss of the child they expected to know and include in activities and interactions with their own families. Each member of the child's family experiences the stages of grief differently and at a different pace.

Stages of Grief

Stages of Grief

Grief is a process. It does not happen in a few days or weeks and then ends. Grief occurs in stages. These stages may overlap and a person may cycle through the grief stages repeatedly. When one family member is at a different grief stage than another, conflict and resentment may occur. Recognizing the stages of grief and which stage you or a loved one is experiencing can help you cope with this process in a more productive way.

Denial

The initial grief stage of denial is frequently associated with feelings of shock, numbness, incapacity to act, and a sense that one is "reeling" from a blow. At such times, a person might think, "this can't be true," "there must be a mistake," "are you sure?" "that doctor doesn't know what she's talking about," or "my child is just putting on an act." Some people experience physical symptoms such as difficulty sleeping, changes in eating habits, feeling dazed, experiencing a hollow feeling in the stomach, or suffering from headaches, constriction in the throat, or weakness. The initial shock and disbelief may be followed by withdrawal from social situations or isolation. Feelings of sadness, anguish, and insistence that the diagnosis of autism is inaccurate may follow. However, some people demonstrate denial by simply continuing their lives as if the diagnosis was never made.

Here are some of the signs that suggest you or your extended family members are in denial following a diagnosis of autism:

- avoiding doing anything to obtain help related to the child's autism;
- avoiding or resisting learning about autism;
- saying or thinking the diagnosis is inaccurate after a second opinion, or continuing to pursue more evaluations to prove it is not autism;
- feeling "paralyzed" and unable to proceed;
- feeling numb or in shock;
- pointing out things the affected loved one does that "proves" it is not autism;
- directing one's energy and efforts toward researching to prove the diagnosis is inaccurate;
- acting as if the diagnosis never happened;
- withdrawal or isolation from others who have accepted the diagnosis.

If you or your loved one is experiencing denial, acknowledge that you currently may feel shock, deep pain, confusion, disbelief, and powerlessness. You have just entered the new and unfamiliar world of autism. Few situations in life are more challenging and emotionally painful than learning your child has autism. Once you recover from the initial shock, the first step is to start learning about autism. Learn the terminology, how your loved one is affected, and what can be done to help him or her grow, learn, and thrive. Learn how to support the child and the immediate family. This is the time to pull together and support one another.

What can I do if I recognize I am in denial or that an extended family member is in denial?

- First, allow yourself and/or your family members' to have the time to react to what they have heard.

- Avoid making any decisions until you stop experiencing physical reactions to what you have been told.

- Recognize that everyone reacts differently. Respect your family members and your own individual reactions. If you or any member of your family needs time alone, try to organize support, so your alone time does not disrupt the family's daily routine. Perhaps a caregiver's services can be arranged to give the family member some much-needed alone time.

- Some people find it helpful to talk to close family or friends at this time. Arrange time to talk with a trusted, supportive family member or friend without children present. It may be necessary to clarify boundaries before talking with a supportive person. Tell the person you just need to talk about what you are feeling. Ask the person to just listen and not make suggestions or offer solutions – just to recognize the person is in pain and needs comfort.

- If you are the trusted family member or friend who is providing support, recognize that the person may be in pain and offer comfort and a sympathetic ear. If it is okay with the grieving person, write down questions based on what the person says, so she can pose those questions to the appropriate resources at a later time. At this point, avoid offering solutions, agreeing or disagreeing with what the grieving person says or offering opinions about her child's symptoms, behaviors, or diagnosis.

- Recognize that everyone's reactions are on a different timetable. Respect your family members' timeframes for reacting and moving to another stage in the grief cycle. Recognize that you may be in a different stage in the grief cycle than they are. When your family member seems to have an annoying attitude regarding your loved one who has autism, step back and think about what stage of the grief cycle they may be experiencing. Understanding the grief stage a family member is experiencing, can help you find constructive ways to respond, instead of feeling annoyed or angry at their reactions. Understanding the grief stage you are experiencing, can help you take constructive actions to move out of that stage and into a more productive pattern of responding.

 CAUTION

Allow yourself time to react. Avoid making any significant decisions or taking action until you have had time to process the initial shock.

- Use the denial in a positive and constructive way. Gather information from reliable sources. Learn more about autism. Share small increments of printed information with family members who are in denial, once they have moved beyond the initial shock and pain.

CASE EXAMPLES

Ella's grandson, Jason, is two years old. When his mother heard he had autism, she was devastated. She cried frequently and insisted the doctors were wrong. She was feeling immense pain and was scared. As her mother, Ella was worried about her daughter and reassured her that she would be there for her. Ella was also grieving about Jason's diagnosis and questioned its accuracy. She began researching reputable websites for information about autism. She found books and other reference materials from reputable publishers. She shared this printed information with her daughter a little at a time, as she seemed ready, so as not to overwhelm her even more. The more Ella and her daughter learned, the more they stopped questioning the diagnosis; instead, they began learning how to help Jason grow and learn, and also sought therapy for him. They have supported each other in their journey to help Jason thrive, even when they did not agree about some things. Together, they have helped Jason by moving from denial to directing their energy and efforts toward helping him and each other.

Uncle Wilson was very concerned about Ty's recent diagnosis of autism. He did not agree with the diagnosis. Ty's mother, Wanda, was Wilson's younger sister. Wanda was so upset and seemed to be in a "fog" following the diagnosis. She was still able to go to work, but could no longer keep up with the laundry or other housework. Wilson wanted to simply tell Wanda the doctors were wrong, so Wanda could return to normal. Instead, Wilson realized he needed to be supportive so he called their other siblings and they each helped in their own way. Wanda's sister came over

(continued)

and listened while Wanda talked about her feelings, and they did laundry together. Wilson watched and fed Ty and his brothers while Wanda and her sister talked. Another sister offered to schedule another appointment with Ty's doctor so they could go together and ask questions to obtain more information.

Anger

Once a family member has moved beyond the denial stage of grief, he or she often becomes angry. The person who took the child for diagnosis or the professional who diagnosed the child may be the one towards whom they direct their anger. Others direct their anger toward the child, a spouse or ex-spouse, parent, other family members, a supreme being, or even another child for being healthy and typical. This anger may flare at sensitive times, such as in meetings with the child's educators or therapists. It is okay to feel angry at this stage, but avoid misdirecting your anger at those who are trying to help you and your loved ones. Grieving family members may quickly alienate friends, family, sources of assistance, and others. Direct your anger into something constructive that can help your loved ones. Develop a strong support network. Direct the energy of your anger into advocating for your family member who has autism.

During the anger stage of grieving you or family members may feel:
- frustrated or jealous;
- anxious or frantic;
- irritable or raging;
- embarrassed or ashamed.

Signs of being in the angry stage of grieving may include:

- Asking "Why me?" "Why my child?" "Why my family?";
- Thinking or saying "It's not fair." "We are good people." "This shouldn't be happening to us." "We don't deserve this.";
- Questioning one's faith or religious/spiritual beliefs regarding a supreme being;
- Self-blame: "This is all my fault. I should not have consumed _____ when I was pregnant.";
- Blaming others: "It's her fault, she didn't talk to him enough.";
- Avoiding taking your loved one with autism out in public anymore;
- Frantically trying to obtain every "cure" and therapy available and being upset if there is a slight delay in starting the treatment.

 CAUTION

Different family members have different perspectives on the child's diagnosis, causes, treatments, and potential outcomes. Family members may be strained and exhausted. They might feel as if they have been left out, their opinions ignored, their needs neglected. Or they may feel disrespected. This is a time when minor disagreements can quickly evolve into major battles. Recognize when someone is experiencing anger as part of grieving and consider using the supports listed.

Supports to consider using when you recognize you or an extended family member is experiencing anger as part of grieving include:

- listening without interrupting. Let them vent. Let them talk about whatever is on their mind.
- recognizing that what is meant as a kind word often infuriates people who are in this stage of grief.

- acting the way you naturally act.
- being patient with the person's mood changes. It's normal for someone who is grieving to move through a variety of emotional extremes.
- showing genuine concern and affection. Give a hug or put your arm around the person's shoulder, if appropriate. If the person is not interested or is irritated that you offered, don't take it personally. Understand that such reactions happen during grieving.
- saying "I'm sorry"; "Tell me how I can help"; "I want to be there for you"; "Would you like a hug?"; "Know that I am here to listen whenever you are ready."
- using creative outlets such as journaling, writing poems, taking photos, or blogging.
- having compassion for family members, the child who has autism, and yourself.

When you recognize you or a family member are in the anger stage of grief:
- Don't avoid the person or isolate yourself. That extended family member (even if it is you) needs love and support at this time.
- Don't pry into personal details.
- Don't ask questions or offer theories about the causes of the child's autism. Don't start talking about how Uncle Bob never talked until he was eight years old.
- Don't say, "I know how you feel."
- Don't say clichés or offer advice or quick solutions.
- Don't try to cheer up the person or distract the person from what he or she is feeling.
- Don't minimize the problem. Don't say, "It's not that bad" or "You'll be okay."
- Don't tell the person how to feel or to stop feeling angry.
- Do say, "I love you" (if you are close enough).

- Do ask "Tell me how I can help?"
- Do say "Tell (the child who has autism and other family members) hi from me," or "Give (the child who has autism and other family members) a big hug for me and tell him I love him."

 CASE EXAMPLE

Mindy had been irritable for several weeks following her daughter Jenny's diagnosis of autism. She was angry and blamed her husband and in-laws for talking her out of having Jenny evaluated sooner. They had convinced Mindy that "everyone in the family was shy." Mindy was so angry at her husband, she would not speak to him except to yell at him when he did not do something the way she expected. She would not look at him or accept any show of affection. She would not respond to him when he spoke to her. Mindy's mother-in-law realized Mindy was grieving. She waited until she was alone with Mindy and quietly told her, "I'm sorry. Tell me how I can help. I love you and Jenny and want to be there for her and for you." A few days later she and Mindy talked and decided to work together to help Jenny grow, learn, and thrive. They talked about how all of them were distraught about Jenny's diagnosis. Mindy's mother-in-law also talked to Mindy's husband to help him understand what Mindy was feeling and to provide support for him. They eventually began having "family meetings" every week to address one another's feelings, concerns, frustrations, and to plan how they could work together to help Jenny.

Bargaining

After a person experiences anger in the grief process, bargaining begins. Family members may start looking for a cure or make promises to a higher power if their child is cured. At this point, the family member will often start reaching out to others with a desire to tell his or her story. The person often struggles to find meaning related to their loved one's diagnosis. Bargaining involves acting or thinking in a manner that prevents or prolongs acceptance of the pain associated with their loved one's diagnosis. Negotiation, often in the form of prayer, may lead the grieving family member to ask for their loved one to be cured or for the diagnosis to be found inaccurate in return for good deeds or for good behavior. In the bargaining stage, you may find yourself overly focused on what you or others could have done differently to prevent your loved one from having autism. Such feelings or accusations related to such feelings can lead to remorse, guilt, and recycling through the anger stage of grieving. Such reactions can interfere with acceptance and healing.

The first step to overcoming the bargaining stage is to recognize what you are saying or doing that is bargaining. Bargaining involves unrealistic reasoning that if you say the right words or complete certain actions, your loved one's autism will go away.

Steps to work through the bargaining stage effectively.

1. Look at the many times you have tried to make a bargain work so your loved one's autism will go away.

During the bargaining stage of grieving, family members may promise:

- "If I do _____, then you will make my loved one not have autism."
- "I will do _____, if you will make my loved one not have autism."

2. Now it is time to face the fact that reality is not going to change. No matter what you do or say, your loved one has autism. There currently is no cure for autism.

3. Once you understand reality is not going to change, make a decision to stop trying to make it change. At this point, you may wish to consider what you can do to help your loved one and your family members accept and effectively address the challenges you all are facing.

4. Keep repeating what you are going to do to address these challenges effectively, instead of spending your energy bargaining for something that is not real. As you do this, you may find that the grief stages of sorrow and anger may surface again, but you will finally arrive at acceptance.

 CASE EXAMPLE

Jesse's stepdaughter, Nadia, was diagnosed with autism when she was three years old. Jesse promised to give more attention to Nadia every day so she would "stop being autistic." Jesse was in the bargaining stage of the grieving process. He and his wife, Jesse's mother, discussed this and he realized he was trying to make bargains to avoid accepting the reality of her diagnosis of autism. He realized that giving Nadia more attention would not make her autism go away. So together they decided Jesse could give Nadia more social play every day to help her learn skills she needed to cope with the effects of autism, rather than trying to make her autism disappear. Jesse realized he could help Nadia grow and learn without making bargains that were unrealistic. As he spent planned time playing with Nadia, Jesse developed a closer relationship with her. He watched as she began responding over time to his social overtures and communication. Nadia began seeking Jesse out in more appropriate ways when she wanted something or needed attention.

Depression

During the depression stage of grieving, final realization of a loss occurs. The child, sibling, niece/nephew, grandchild, or other relative you are sharing life with and helping grow up is different to the child you had dreamed of or anticipated. You may experience a profound feeling of loss, sadness, hopelessness, or overwhelming despair. This is not the life you dreamed of. This is not the family you had hoped for. Autism is 24/7. There is no break from autism's effects. This sense of loss, sadness, and despair can become even more exaggerated by a loss of restful sleep when living with a child affected by autism who has difficulty sleeping at night.

To help you get through this stage:
- take some time away from autism, even if only for a few hours;
- make arrangements with a sitter, trusted friend, or family member so you can take a break;
- cry, give yourself some time to feel sad, then pamper yourself;
- call a supportive, positive friend;
- do something you enjoy;
- consider talking to a counselor or therapist.

CASE EXAMPLE

Brandon's grandmother, Nani, and mother, Mami, were very close. They were both devastated when Brandon was diagnosed with autism. After a few months, both Nani and Mami were exhausted from pursuing so many different interventions, therapies, and doctors' appointments. Additionally, they were exhausted from taking turns each night to get up with Brandon when he was awake. They began to realize nothing they could do would make Brandon's autism go away. They both became very sad and depressed. Brandon's aunt was very concerned about them. She sat down with them to create a schedule in 24-hour periods that was arranged so one person would get up every time Brandon was awake each night. That person was "assigned" to deal with any behavior problems that occurred during the assigned 24-hour period. The other person was allowed to sleep through the night, did not have the responsibility of responding to behavior problems for the designated 24-hour period, and could come and go from the home to run errands or enjoy some pampering.

Acceptance

Acceptance is the final stage in the grief cycle. Acceptance is recognizing the pain of a loss, coming to terms with that loss, and being ready to move beyond it. To reach acceptance, the person has taken the steps necessary to go on with life while understanding and accepting that a loss has occurred. During the stage of acceptance, a person regains a sense of hope, thinks creatively about the future, lets go of the illusion of being able to control the pain associated with the loss, and realizes that life can still continue, though it will be different than before the loss.

When grieving a diagnosis of autism, stages of grief are often experienced in a repeating cycle.

acceptance   **denial**

depression
                                    anger

bargaining

However, it is important to recognize that many people skip stages and repeat stages they previously experienced. People do not always go through each stage in the same order. Sometimes people never seem to go through denial, but straight to bargaining or anger.

If a family member is experiencing the grieving cycle you can help by:

- Acting naturally. Acting uncomfortable or different is often hard on the person who is grieving.
- Allow the person to talk about their feelings. Listen without interrupting or talking about you.
- Be patient with the person's changing moods.
- Show genuine concern and affection if the person appears to be open to it. If the person seems distant or uninterested, do not take it personally.
- Be silent if the person prefers it. Simply sit silently beside the person.
- Be specific in your offers to help.

Take the initiative to:

- stop by and check on the person to see if he/she needs anything;
- call just to talk or to check on the person;
- drop off food without being asked;
- stop by and babysit so the main caretaker can have a break and some time for herself or himself;
- offer to accompany the person to appointments with doctors, teachers, or other professionals;
- offer to go with him/her to support groups or a bereavement group;
- accompany the person on walks or enjoy a physical activity together
- do a fun activity that you know he/she enjoys, such as a game or going to the movies;
- offer to take the person's child out for an activity so the person can have some time alone at home;
- when the person is ready, encourage socializing;
- lend a hand. Wash dishes or clothes. Cook a meal. Help with errands.

Understand How Autism Affects Relationships within the Family

Communication and relationships are the building blocks that create a family's foundation. Your loved one was diagnosed with autism because of communication, social, and behavioral challenges that interfere significantly with building and maintaining relationships. This affects every relationship in the family, along with the entire manner in which the family and extended family function.

Social challenges in autism that affect relationships with the person who has autism may include:

- limited or unusual responses to other people;
- interactions with others to obtain desired items or control events;
- extreme interaction styles with others: unfriendly or too friendly;
- difficulty "reading" and responding appropriately to social cues;
- showing greater interest/attachment to objects than family members;
- inappropriate, disruptive, or dangerous behavior that interferes with family members' life, work, school, or relationships;
- limited emotional understanding;
- difficulty tolerating or joining in social activities.

How to Cope as a Family after a Diagnosis of Autism

Mothers and Fathers

In the first few years, mothers might doubt themselves and worry about the future as significant challenges arise for their child with autism. These challenges may include diarrhea, constipation, behavioral challenges, irritability, and sleep problems, which can affect everyone in the household. Is it any wonder that with all of this, the fabric of the family is precariously stretched? This is the time to look closely at the family to ensure that each member's needs are addressed. This is not an easy task when the fog of disbelief and despair often mar good judgment. Stress adds to the situation, although some partners become even closer as result of the unique experience of raising a child with ASD.

Parents rarely grieve the same way and at the same pace, yet couples often expect to process grief together, which is unrealistic and can result in even more stress. One parent may want to talk it out while the other may prefer to be alone and go walking in the hills. Intimacy can be stretched to breaking point.

Some parents want to read books or start therapy with the child. The other parent may simply want to be a friend and try to live as "normally" as possible. Some look at every moment as an opportunity to learn, a sentiment their partner may not share. One parent might want to try alternative or experimental treatment, while the other parent might be keen to try more traditional treatments first.

Although some relationships may weaken in the process, facts indicate the prevalence of divorce among parents of children with autism is much lower than previously thought.

Some moms might be too proud or embarrassed to acknowledge their need for help and support. Others recite self-affirmations, "I have strength, I have power, I am smart – I can figure this out, I can learn, I can do this." For others, seeing a counselor can be extremely beneficial.

Few dads have opportunities to meet with doctors and therapists as often as mothers. They may appear stoic and even more withdrawn, sometimes to avoid conflicts in their children's care that they do not fully understand or agree with. In one fathers' group, the pain and devastation impacting dads became starkly apparent despite some initial denial of the diagnosis, its severity, and impact on family functioning.

This is the time parents need to be reminded or to remind themselves that they are also wives and husbands. Roles played by fathers and mothers change and often become more traditional. Mothers might spend more time at home, involved with the child, while fathers might be at work providing economic support. Of course, that is not always the case as traditional roles are often reversed. The demands single parents face certainly have to be twice as challenging.

Treatment options are often controversial and can lead to conflicts between parents. One or both parents might even question the diagnosis. Finances can be greatly affected and may quickly become strained. Parents are often stressed, worried, and exhausted, and might feel neglected and disrespected. Resentment can quickly arise in these situations.

Each parent responds very differently; some are problem solvers and seek action; others need time and opportunities to express emotions. Fathers and mothers can have different perspectives on the causes of, and treatments available for, autism and even the prognosis, all of which can lead to misunderstandings. This is a time that minor issues can intensify into major conflicts. Having a supportive family network becomes more important than ever!

Accepting, understanding, and coping with a diagnosis of autism is never easy. Every family copes differently when presented with this diagnosis. Some families are devastated, while other families are relieved that their concerns have been validated. Some families seek out support immediately while other families might close in and become home bound or even reclusive.

Extended family members can develop positive social relationships with loved ones who have autism, in spite of the person's underlying social and communication limitations. How those relationships are developed and expressed may look very different than the relationships they have with other family members.

CHAPTER 4

Grandparents

Grandparents are among the most important people in their grandchildren's lives, including grandchildren with autism. Grand parenting a child with autism can be very challenging, but also very rewarding. Grandparents usually know a lot about children. However, it is often difficult and confusing for grandparents to understand what is happening to the grandchild they were dying to spoil.

Grandparents can be the easiest or hardest family members to deal with when a child is diagnosed with autism. Doctors just love it when grandparents accompany their own children and their precious grandchild to the clinic. Invariably, they add an enormous amount of moral support, assistance, and positive perspectives. Although they can often seem to be in denial of the reality of the situation, on the other hand they can be more accepting of the situation in general and the dreaded label in particular, than any other family member. The wisdom gained from years of experience has taught them what is important, how to maintain perspective, and how to establish priorities. Most parents rely heavily on their grandparents and often say they don't know how they would ever cope without them!

A grandchild with autism will change your life. Grandchildren with autism need you:

- to be a safe person in a confusing, overwhelming world;
- to be flexible, compassionate, and supportive when they appear to be misbehaving;
- to listen and respect them when they communicate they do not want to do something;
- to accommodate their special needs;
- to love them.

As discussed earlier, parents can often be in denial as well – not necessarily consciously, of course, but the recognition of challenges within a child is often just too painful. Grandparents often ask how to broach concerns about their grandchild when their own children seem to refuse to acknowledge the gravity of the situation. Sometimes parents indirectly rely on observations from other significant people in the child's life to work out or process their own concerns about their child. They might not always state it that way! Not that they will necessarily act on the concerns of others, such as schoolteachers and family friends, but at least they hear it, digest it, and later put it in context. Eventually, the seriousness of the problem will become apparent and it is usually then that the parents will seek a diagnostic evaluation. So a grandparent's input might just be a cog in the wheel of the diagnostic process. They should take comfort from knowing that their children will have to learn through their own experiences what is going on and what needs to be done!

Just as parents were their own individuals before having children, so were you, dear grandparents! And grandparents must recognize there might still be unresolved issues between themselves and their children. These do not necessarily resolve themselves just because there is a grandchild with autism. On the other hand, a crisis in the family can sometimes serve as an opportunity for resolution and end up strengthening the entire extended family structure. It will require the delineation of good boundaries, roles, and attitudes. But this is time for the tough to get going; to dig deep into one's soul and come up with coping mechanisms, insights, and perspectives that might have been elusive for some time. This indeed could be a wonderful healing opportunity on many levels; most importantly, it might allow grandparents to be those very special people in the life of their grandchild

So what can grandparents do?

- Not everything that worked with your own children may work with your family member who has autism. Learn all you can about autism. Be creative in finding ways to support your grandchild, his parents, and siblings.
- You are your children's most precious natural resource. Do you understand the grieving your child is experiencing? Are you yourself going through any of this now? Remember the "Welcome to Holland" story. Emily Perl Kingsley compared having a child with autism to landing up in Holland when you were planning to travel to Italy. If you

spend the rest of your life mourning the fact that you didn't get to see Italy, you may never be free to enjoy the very special, lovely things about Holland.

- You can be your child's best advocate and stress reducer. You can come through on their behalf and help your child through the process.

Opportunities for grandparents and others to get involved!
- Educate yourself about the symptoms, the diagnostic process, the treatments, the educational programs, the insurance issues.
- Review "Welcome to the World of Autism" in Chapter 2.
- Learn your grandchild's strengths and weaknesses!
- Attend office visits. Ask permission of course. Offer to serve as a note-taker.
- Keep files straight – once again, ask for permission.
- Sit in the back – don't just do something, sit there!
- Get or create autism explanation cards to hand to strangers who might not understand. This is a way of explaining your grandchild's disability and behaviors. Hand them out often! Everyone needs to learn more!
- Need to read a good book on Autism? See Appendix J for a list of recommended titles.
- Create an Autism Care Tool Kit (see Activity C).

Parents are not the only family members who create an expectation of the "perfect child" in their imagination. Grandparents can also have an expectation of the "perfect grandchild." A diagnosis of autism is often the last expectation any grandparent or parent imagines or expects to hear. Once the diagnosis is made, the expectation of a "perfect grandchild" is shattered. Often a grandparent will simply ignore the diagnosis, pretending nothing is wrong. Others may feel a storm of strong emotion such as guilt, blame, anger, fear, and confusion. Such emotions can be overwhelming. No two grandparents respond the same when they hear their grandchild has autism. As a grandparent of a child who has autism, you will likely experience grief following your grandchild's diagnosis. Please review the section on the grief process in Chapter 3 and familiarize yourself with what to expect and how best to cope.

Once you have worked past some of the raw overwhelming emotions and feel you are ready to begin to accept your grandchild's diagnosis, focus on learning about autism. Within the framework of information you learn about autism, learn to identify your grandchild's individual strengths and needs. Always remember he or she is a person who just happens to have autism.

Grandparents often experience a second source of grief when a grandchild has been diagnosed with autism. Grandparents are the parents of that child's parents. Grandparents grieve for their own child who will not have the same parenting experiences the grandparent had in raising them. They grieve for their own child who is facing a lifetime of challenges that come with having a child with autism. Grandparents don't only worry and grieve for themselves; they worry and grieve for their own adult child's loss and future also.

CAUTION

Avoid trying to rush through the grieving process. Everyone grieves at a different pace and in a different way. Grandparents' grieving process may be extended since they are not only grieving for their grandchild who has autism; they are likely grieving for their adult child, their other adult children, and their other grandchildren, all of whom have been affected. Allow yourself the time you need to sort through your feelings before making any decisions about how to proceed. However, eventually it is important to stop grieving and start living and enjoying your grandchild.

The most important step to take next is to gain power through knowledge. Educate yourself about autism. Different generations were raised with different attitudes towards disabilities. They might have a different attitude towards disabilities and some might prefer to avoid labels or a diagnosis completely. That confusion can often result in conflict. Grandparents also need education. Maybe their children need to write them a letter and include comments such as "You're babying the child; you are not being firm enough." These comments may leave them cold, but it may provide the right incentive for them to help. There is certainly lots they can do!

These different attitudes can lead to conflicts between parents and grandparents. To grow beyond any limitations of the attitudes you learned about disabilities, learn current, quality information about autism. Grandparents can add an enormous amount of support, assistance, and positive perspectives. The wisdom gained from years of experience has taught you what is important, how to maintain perspective, and how to establish priorities.

Learning all you can about autism and your grandchild as a unique individual is the key to being the best grandparent you can for your grandchild with autism. You can help and support your family effectively when you understand the problems your adult child, your grandchild, and other family members are facing. Avoid simply relying on your adult child to provide you with information about autism. Seek out information independently (See Appendix J for a list of recommended information resources).

 CASE EXAMPLE

Nana was devastated when she was told her grandson, Joey, had autism. She cried inconsolably for days. Then she insisted that the doctor was mistaken; there was nothing wrong with Joey. Nana decided that Joey was just a late talker who had a great imagination and was spoiled. She loved Joey so much. When Nana seemed to have no more tears to cry she decided she had to help her daughter, Joey's mother. Although she did not agree with the diagnosis, Nana decided to learn all she could about autism. She had to admit that her initial goal in learning about autism was to prove the doctor wrong. However, the more she read about autism, the more she realized Joey and his mother needed her even more. She realized that Joey's "tantrums," demanding behaviors, refusal to eat what others were eating, wandering about the house at night, late talking, and "imaginative play" were all related to his autism. Nana learned how to communicate and play with Joey, how to recognize, respect, and improve his tolerance limits, and how to enter into his imaginative world to play with him. She also became a source of support and comfort to Joey's older siblings.

Your grandchild with autism will change your life. You have the power to determine whether that change will be positive or negative. In your role as grandparent, your relationship with your grandchild is your priority. The better you understand your grandchild who has autism, the better your relationship will be. Educate yourself and learn how to interact with your grandchild in a way that is best suited to his needs.

You can support your grandchild by:

- Learning all you can about autism and your grandchild's unique strengths and needs.
- Putting your grandchild's needs first.
- Avoiding babying or spoiling your grandchild. Learn the best ways to meet the child's needs while keeping his future success in mind.
- Avoiding being too demanding, critical, or harsh.
- Understanding and providing what your grandchild needs to be able to regain or maintain acceptable behaviors.
- Learning how to communicate effectively with your grandchild.
- Providing other forms of support if or when you are unable or too uncomfortable to directly interact with your grandchild for extended periods.

CASE EXAMPLE

Grampa Carlos was not comfortable around children. His granddaughter, Maria, had been diagnosed with autism. Maria loved to climb, run, and wander. She loved water, but had no concept of safety. One time she escaped out of the back door, climbed over the fence and disappeared for more than an hour. Grampa Carlos and Maria's parents searched for her and finally found her near a pond in the neighborhood. Maria's parents frequently had to intervene when she repeatedly opened doors, windows, and cabinets. Grampa Carlos did not know what to say or do when Maria was around, so he would simply greet her then direct his attention to the adults in the area. He did this with all of his grandchildren. Grampa Carlos loved his grandchildren. He especially wanted to help his son, Maria's father, because he realized the extra responsibilities Maria's parents were facing. Grampa Carlos decided to help them by doing what he did best; he helped with environmental modifications to the house to help keep Maria calm and safe. He installed safety locks on the cabinets, windows, and doors; safety equipment to protect Maria from accessing the stove and oven; gates to prevent access to off- limits areas of the house; and alarms on the doors and windows. Once Maria's environment was safe, he built a play area in the backyard so she could enjoy climbing in an appropriate way. Grampa Carlos also arranged for Maria to obtain swimming lessons so she could be safe if she was ever near water again.

Tips from Grandparents

- My grandson has autism. Going to some of his therapy sessions really helped me understand what was going on with him and to find better ways to help him.

- We have two grandchildren who have autism and one who has Asperger's. The most important thing we do for them is to let them know we are there for them and that they are loved so very much.

- I attend family counseling sessions with my daughter and her husband so we can learn how to work together to help my granddaughter who has autism.

- I have a rambunctious ten-year-old grandson, who is big and has autism. He does not realize how easily he can hurt me. I cannot be around him alone, but I provide other support in the form of doing research and learning as much as I can to pass on to my son and his wife.

- Never give up!!! Research, ask questions, and make phone calls.

- I cannot stand or walk for more than one minute or so, due to bad knees. I go to my daughter's house three days every week to fold her laundry and mend clothes, which she greatly appreciates.

- Our home is not a safe environment for our grandson who has autism. Therefore, every other Friday night we stay at my daughter and son-in-law's house so they can have a "date night." Sometimes they stay at our house for the night and come home the next day.

- I am a retired certified swim instructor. I taught all of my grandchildren how to swim, and take them to a pool periodically (along with their parents) to make sure they remember how to swim and to teach them pool safety.

- We live in another country far away from our grandchild who has autism and thus cannot visit very often. But we visit with all our grandchildren every week on Skype.

- I have two grandchildren. One has autism and the other one does not. I make sure that I provide a listening ear and a comforting shoulder for my other grandchild who does not have autism. She needs to be heard and needs support in her struggles to cope with her brother's outbursts and aggression.

CHAPTER 5

How are Siblings Impacted by Extended Family Matters?

A lthough siblings are not members of the extended family, they play a significant role in the interaction between extended family members and their loved one who has autism. Brothers and sisters within the immediate family unquestionably experience the stresses of the family as a whole and are also affected by the fact that the parents are focusing on the child with autism, which may lead to siblings feeling neglected. Brothers and sisters need to have autism demystified through developmentally appropriate explanations and education. As an extended family member you play a role in helping siblings understand autism and how it affects their brother or sister. Include siblings in activities for the child with autism. If you are supporting a family member by attending therapies and office visits, consider including the child's siblings in those therapies and office visits. Siblings need recognition, understanding, and guidance related to the emotional complexities they experience; these may include anger, resentment, embarrassment, and/or fear. Consider taking the sibling to a sibling support program, which can provide a wonderful opportunity for siblings to meet others having similar experiences, realize they are not alone, and that other siblings also experience many of the thoughts and fears they are experiencing. Most importantly, siblings need to feel loved, wanted, and heard.

Because of genetic inheritance patterns, siblings have a higher chance of having autism or more commonly, experiencing other subtle developmental difficulties, such as language learning disabilities and anxiety disorders. In addition, there are adjustment issues. Parents might over-focus on the affected child with unintended neglect of a sibling.

What can extended family members do to help siblings?
- Give them a voice. Acknowledge their spoken or unspoken concerns.
- Include siblings in therapies and office visits. It's great when they attend!
- It demystifies the "special" times they might think their sibling have during these appointments.
- Ask the doctor, therapist, or other service provider to address the sibling directly. Siblings need recognition!
- Know that siblings experience emotions such as anger, resentment, embarrassment, fear, guilt, and/or jealousy related to experiences involving their brother or sister who has autism.
- Validate their feelings. It's normal to have those negative feelings. Validating their emotions can help to decrease negative feelings.

- Consider taking the sibling(s) to a sibling support program. These programs present a wonderful opportunity for siblings to meet others and hear that they are not alone. Discussion at these groups can center around self-esteem, teasing, stress management, communication skill development, and learning about autism.

 CASE EXAMPLE

Zack had ABA therapy at a therapy center and at home three days a week. His mother was present during sessions at home and his grandmother took him to his sessions at the therapy center. In therapy Zack worked on learning how to play rather than persistently fixating on repeatedly watching the same show on TV, the computer, phone, tablet, or reader at every opportunity. Zack's older sister, Erika, was a little quirky and had limited social skills. Her social skills were not as limited as Zack's; however, when they tried to play together or were in the same room with one another, Erika would eventually begin screaming at Zack and sometimes hit or shove him. Zack would try to take all of the toys away from Erika or would simply ignore or scream at her. Then Erika would try to cue Zack the same way she heard their mother tell him what to do and Zack would either ignore her or scream at her. Erika was very jealous of the attention Zack received during therapy and repeatedly interrupted sessions. Sometimes she had to sit and wait in the therapy play area while Zack got to play. During therapy sessions at home, Erika watched while Zack worked with his therapist to learn how to play with a variety of toys. Zack's therapist talked to their mother and grandmother about ways to include Erika in part of Zack's therapy sessions. During the first portion of Zack's sessions, he worked on learning or practicing social skills and/

(continued)

or play behaviors; then Erika was included so they could practice the same skills together. Their mother reported they were actually starting to play together in an acceptable manner at home. Screaming and aggression decreased, and within months were rarely occurring. Erika stopped acting jealous of Zack and the therapist eventually taught her how to cue Zack in such a way that he cooperated with her.

Siblings may have many worries and/or stress related to their brother or sister who has autism. Such worries and stress can be very unsettling for siblings who are still children and for those who have already reached adulthood.

Worries that siblings have may include:

- Sometimes siblings worry about the future of their brother or sister who has autism. Older siblings may also worry about how their lives will be affected by possibly having to care for or be responsible for a brother or sister who has autism.
- Siblings are often affected by stress, confusion, embarrassment, fear of being bullied by other children, and fear of being verbally taunted by their brother or sister.
- Siblings may resent not being able to go to the movies, shopping, parties, visiting relatives or family friends, or going on vacations due to the disruptive behaviors of their brother or sister who has autism. Siblings may be disappointed they don't have a brother or sister to play with.
- Siblings often resent the additional attention their brother or sister with autism receives or the additional support their brother or sister receives.
- Siblings may feel obligated to avoid asking for something they want because they do not want to cause their parents additional stress.

- Siblings may not realize they are experiencing worry or stress related to their brother or sister with autism. Or they may realize they are having negative feelings toward their family or brother or sister with autism, but do not want to tell anyone about it.

How can I tell when a sibling is worried or stressed if they do not tell someone, and what can we do to help?

- The sibling is acting out in order to attract more attention from his/her parents or other family members, or acts sullen or angry when a brother or sister receives special attention or accommodations. Make a special effort to take the time to give the sibling special individual attention. Consider making "dates" with the sibling to do something exclusively with him or her. Consider babysitting or providing a caretaker for the child with autism so the parent can have a special "date" or "alone time" with the sibling. This time need not be lengthy. It can be as short as a scheduled story at bedtime or an hour outing on the weekend.
- The sibling complains about not being special, not being given special consideration, or having fewer privileges or more restrictions than the brother or sister who has autism. Be sure to tell and show the sibling that he or she is unique and special. Recognize and show gratitude when the sibling's routine or expectation is altered to accommodate a brother or sister with autism.
- The sibling complains no one listens to or cares about him or her. Include the sibling in family discussions, tasks, and decisions. Teach him or her that fair does not mean equal; it means providing the supports each individual needs to be successful.

CASE EXAMPLE

Danny is eight years old, has autism, is nonverbal, and is frequently physically aggressive. His older brother, Mark, is in middle school. Danny enjoys watching his favorite cartoons, which are recorded for viewing on the TV in the family room. Danny has the daily routine of playing outside after school or on weekend mornings. When he finishes playing, he watches his favorite cartoons on the TV in the family room. When he has to stay indoors but cannot watch his cartoons on TV, he becomes angry and often attacks his family. Danny does not have any other leisure skills for indoors. Mark can only play his favorite video games on the TV in the family room. Mark resents Danny always being given preferential treatment by being allowed to have first choice to use the TV in the family room. His parents are just trying to minimize Danny's physical aggression so they can have a peaceful evening or weekend at home. Since Mark is older and does not have autism, they expect him to understand. Mark's grandmother offered to have Mark come to her house a couple of evenings each week and for a couple of hours every other Saturday so he could enjoy his video games undisturbed. Danny's ABA therapist began teaching him a wider variety of indoor leisure activities. They practiced these activities every session in Danny's bedroom while the TV was on in the family room, so they became routine for him. Eventually Danny's therapist had Mark play his video game while Danny played his newly learned activities in his bedroom. They eventually posted a picture schedule that showed where Danny would be and where Mark would be during leisure time. Danny began tolerating Mark playing video games on the TV in the family room during his scheduled times.

What else can extended family do to help siblings of a child who has autism?

Encourage the parents to tell the siblings about their brother or sister's diagnosis in a way that is appropriate for the sibling's age and developmental level to help everyone who is affected understand their brother or sister's behaviors and needs.

Find special time for siblings. It's impossible to provide children with exactly the same amount of attention, particularly when one or more of those children have autism. Individualize your attention and the time spent with each child to fit that child's unique needs and tolerance limits, rather than trying to keep the time spent with each child and the activities equal. Children tend to remember having fun with you, rather than "keeping score." If a child is "keeping score," explore this issue further; it usually masks underlying resentments related to the attention or special treatment their sibling receives, rather than actually being solely about that particular event.

Set up a "men's or "women's" hour once a week during which the boys meet with family members who are men or the girls meet with family members who are women. This can be a great time to discuss feelings and ways to cope. Don't ask, pry, or lecture; simply share your own feelings from when you were a child about embarrassment, pride, jealousy, fears, and other feelings. A day before your "session," think of one or two scenarios you can recall from your childhood. Be sure to select feelings that lead to positive guidance. Avoid using these meetings to complain or air your own unresolved grievances from childhood. Keep in mind these meetings should have the goal of helping your child learn that such feelings are normal and how to cope in a constructive way. Use a storytelling approach, rather than a more direct form of teaching.

You have permission to spend time without all family members. This includes, but is not limited to, restaurants, outings, parties, holiday events, weddings, funerals, and even vacations. Avoid treating children the same way when they are inherently not the same; and remember, they have different tolerance limits and preferences. Be practical and consider individual tolerance limits and preferences before taking all the children to the same events. For example, the circus can be great fun for some and excruciating torture for others. These situations present great opportunities for extended family members to spend quality time with their relatives by taking one or more of the children on an outing without taking disinterested siblings on that particular outing.

 CASE EXAMPLE

Chase found restaurants intolerable. The mix of different smells, the noise, and too many people being nearby and talking over one another was so overwhelming Chase was unable to eat. Chase's mother wanted to respect this so she let Chase stay with her best friend when she and Chase's father and siblings went out to eat. Chase enjoyed eating his favorite food and having time to engage in his favorite activities without disruption. His mother's friend lets Chase enjoy his favorite activities while his family enjoys a meal out.

CASE EXAMPLE

Uncle Luis and Aunt Lisa have two sons who are younger than their cousin with autism, Miguel, and one son the same age as Miguel. Miguel does not have any friends his age. He does not like the same activities that his same-age cousin likes. He wants friends, but his interests are similar to those of much younger children. One day Aunt Lisa and Miguel's mother were visiting and talking about their children. They realized Miguel and Aunt Lisa's younger children enjoyed being outdoors playing in the park and on the playground equipment at the park. They had not considered having the boys play together since they were so many years apart in age. They made a play date and met at the park. Miguel played with his cousins and all three boys had a fun time. Miguel's mother was so excited to have found some playmates for Miguel. They began meeting regularly at the park and on rainy days they met at Miguel or Aunt Lisa's house. The boys discovered other activities they enjoyed doing together. Miguel's mother taught his cousins what Miguel acted like when he needed a quiet break away from talking, people, and playing. They learned what to do and say when Miguel needed those breaks. Now, after taking a break, Miguel rejoins the fun on his own. He is happy to have his cousins as his friends, too.

CHAPTER 6

Stepfamilies and Other Blended Families

B lending families together can be a rewarding, yet challenging experience. Blended families are typically thought to consist of a couple joining together and combining their respective children into one family. In these types of blended families, there are usually children from one or both of the couple's previous relationships. However, there are other forms of blended families. Some blended families consist of friends, adult siblings, or other adult relatives living together in one household with their respective children. Other types of blended families may consist of a grandparent, both grandparents, and/or other relatives coming together to share a household, often blending their own children into that household. Some blended families include foster siblings. When at least one of the children in the blended family has autism, the challenges may be intensified. The children involved in blended families may resist such changes. Some adults may also resist the changes that usually accompany such a significant change in daily life. Step-parents or other adults in the household may become frustrated when their new, blended family does not function as expected. The affected children may not know one another very well, may not get along, may have difficulty tolerating others, or may not even like one another.

It is important to recognize that changes to family structure and daily routines require adjustments for everyone involved, particularly with a child with autism. Every child is different and will show you through his or her behavior how slow or fast to proceed, as all of you grow and develop into a family unit. Some children are more open and flexible. Some children are more willing to become engaged with new family members. In time, through patience, interest, respect, and support, most children and adults will eventually accept their new blended family.

Step-parents will hopefully have had many opportunities for getting to know the child, and to understand the potential challenges. Just like any extended family member, step-parents need to understand issues basic to ASD, such as what behavior means. For example, realize that behavior has a communicative intent and avoid assuming that a stepchild's behavior is directed at anyone personally. Also, blaming a spouse for the child's actions is counterproductive and unhelpful. Most importantly, never underestimate the destructive impact of negative talk directed towards the child, even if he or she is acting belligerent. Some decisions are best deferred to the biological parents.

Step-parents might be called, PBC (a parent by choice), which is similar to a parent adopting a child. Parents of children with autism are often heard to say, "I have no choice" when praised by others for the tough job they have. Step-parents had that choice and need to be supported in their roles as a PBC!

When blending families that include a child who has autism:

- Teach other family members about autism and the family member who has autism.
- Maintain as much of the child's daily routine as possible.
- Use visual schedules prior to and following the family blending together, so the routine is to follow the schedule, not to complete memorized activities in a particular order and location.
- Provide a "safe place" to which the child can retreat when needed or scheduled. Ideally, have this in place so it is familiar before the move.

Single parents and extended family members

For single parents, parent friendships might take the place of spouses and/or biological extended family members. "Adoptive" aunts, uncles, or grandparents can be wonderful sources of support. There are so many aspects to raising a child with autism, and any assistance is likely to be welcomed. Activities such as baby-sitting, running errands, doing the laundry, Internet research, providing transportation, along with many other forms of support, can be asked for but ideally will be offered.

Parents, especially single parents, often say things like:

- I don't have friends who "get it" and support me or accept me.
- It's not fair to be told to "make sure you make time for yourself" when I don't have time to do anything differently.
- Others tell me to get a babysitter. What if no one wants to take care of a child with aggressive behavior?

In divorce situations, issues such as consistency and lack of adherence to treatment programs frequently arise. Establishing good lines of communication and even using an Individual Parents Plan (IPP) can help to facilitate a workable co-parenting plan.

 CASE EXAMPLE

Bailey was five when his parents divorced. His father and mother disagreed about how to address his behaviors. Bailey's father tried to work with him and kept in frequent contact with his teachers and therapists. Bailey's mother came to pick him up every two through four months for a weekend visit. Bailey's ABA therapist wrote up simple steps that showed how to communicate these visits to Bailey, so he would not become upset and refuse to go with his mother or return to his father. The therapist showed the parents how to use a picture calendar and a picture schedule along with a picture exchange communication system so Bailey could understand when and how visits began and ended and could communicate more effectively with his parents. When Bailey's behavior improved, his parents realized what he needed. The therapist continued teaching them how to help Bailey be successful, a goal shared by both of Bailey's parents.

So step-parents get involved! Here's what you can do!

- Education is key – you are reading this book for that very reason. Review the sections on the key challenges autism poses.
- Attend meetings at school and, with permission, doctor visits as well.
- Remember some decisions are best deferred to the biological parents.
- Be mindful! Meditate on the need for patience and seeing your step-child as part of the whole situation and not according to any of your own ideas as to how they should be. This is good advice for all parents.
- Be your own pillar and let the wind of heaven blow between you and your new spouse.
- Of course you will make mistakes; of course you will get things wrong. It's only out of involvement that mistakes happen and learning begins. The cracks are where the light gets in, says Leonard Cohen!
- Learn about behavior and its communicative intent. Never assume your stepchild's behavior is about you, even if it is directed at you. It's important for all parents not to take things personally.
- Avoid shaming and blaming feelings.

See **Activity D** - How to communicate well as a step-parent.

Strengthen a blended family by:

- creating clear, safe boundaries, with the biological parent being the disciplinarian and the other adults acting as friends or counselors;
- creating a list of family rules;
- being consistent and predictable;
- communicating often and openly;
- listening respectfully to one another;
- using routines, rituals, and your own family traditions to bond;
- showing affection;
- doing activities together as a family unit while respecting the needs of the child who has autism.

 CAUTION

When blending families, the adults and children involved may experience a period of grieving as they have "lost" the daily lives, routines, and family interactions previously experienced. There may be additional difficulties related to one or more of the children having already experienced a trusted loved one "letting them down" when previous relationships ended or changed. Although the child with autism may not be able to express these feelings adequately or in the same way as other children, he or she may still experience anxiety related to previous learning regarding trust and relationships with adults.

Creating family routines, rituals, and traditions helps unite a family. Routines, rituals, and traditions can also be comforting to a child who has autism especially if that child prefers predictable events and activities. Decide on meaningful family rituals that already exist in one or both of the families being blended together and incorporate at least one of those rituals into your newly blended family. These rituals might include weekend visits to the beach, a weekly game night, a weekly movie night, Saturday night pizza, or regular family meals. Be sure to include a family routine your child with autism can enjoy or, at the very least, tolerate. The activity may need to be modified to accommodate his or her tolerance limits.

Maintain your relationship with your spouse or significant other by:
- Setting aside time as a couple by making regular dates or meeting for lunch or coffee during school time.
- Presenting a unified parenting approach to the children. Any disagreement should be discussed away from the children or other adults living in the home who may try to take sides or come between you.
- Model love, respect, and open, positive communication to help your children feel more secure and learn those skills.

Tips for a healthy blended family:
- Recognize that children adjust to blended families differently at different ages.
- Recognize that all siblings have conflicts, so don't assume that family arguments are always the result of a blended family or one child having autism.
- Make special arrangements for each child to have his or her own private space for personal items.
- Locate a support group or consider counseling if a child continues to display resentment, anger, or loss of pleasure from enjoyable activities; or if an adult in the home openly favors one child over another.

Keep all parents involved. Children will adjust better in blended family situations if they have access to both biological parents. It is important for all parents to be involved and working toward a parenting partnership. Tell the children you and their other biological parents love them and will continue to love them and be available for them throughout their lives. Be sure your children understand that your new partner is not a replacement mother or father, but an additional person who will love and support them.

 CASE EXAMPLE

Auntie Billie and her teenage son, Wiley, came to live with her sister, Kathy, and her son, Jessie, a 10 year old boy who has autism. Wiley loved to play loud music, which upset Jessie because he was accustomed to having a quiet home setting with no music playing. Jessie began having aggressive "meltdowns" during which he broke objects in the house, screamed, wailed, and tore up Wiley's belongings. Auntie Billie and Kathy thought Jessie was angry and jealous that another child was living in his home. However, they began to notice that Jessie would have meltdowns when Wiley played his music loudly. Kathy explained to Auntie Billie and Wiley that Jessie used to be overly sensitive to noises, but thought he had "outgrown it" since he no longer put his fingers in his ears as he used to. Auntie Billie pointed out that Kathy had probably simply accommodated Jessie by creating a quiet environment. They decided that Wiley needed to use headphones when playing his music, but they also wanted Jessie to learn to tolerate reasonable noise, so they began playing soft music occasionally in the background at home. As Jessie began tolerating the music, they gradually increased the volume and times the music played.

CASE EXAMPLE

Lisa and Tony were engaged to be married. Lisa had a son, Marco, who had autism. Tony had two sons who were neurotypical. Prior to marrying and moving into the same home, Lisa and Tony prepared for the changes that were about to take place. Tony asked questions and tried to understand what Marco was experiencing and how to approach and support him. Lisa shared as much information about autism with Tony and his sons as she could. Tony spent individual time with Marco to develop a relationship with him without extra distractions. They both spoke with Tony's sons about what Marco needed to feel safe and secure. They taught Tony's sons how to use Marco's communication book and what types of activities he liked. They planned time to spend together as a family and time for Marco to be away from people, which he needed regularly. They also planned time for Tony to spend with his sons. Lisa and Tony joined a local support group for parents of children who have autism. They obtained respite services for Marco, so they could have a date night every Friday and occasionally a weekend getaway.

So when behavior challenges get in the way, make sure you learn appropriate behavior management strategies. Ask your autism therapist or ABA therapist for help in this area. They are the experts!

Please see **Activity F** - Behavior Management for Extended Family Members for extra tips.

CHAPTER 7

Uncles and Aunts

Being an aunt or uncle is a privilege. Enhance that relationship with your niece or nephew who has autism so that it is as loving, meaningful, impactful, and positive as possible. Also understand that your sister or brother who has a child with autism still needs the loving support of all his or her brothers and sisters. At this time, their relationship with their own child who has autism is likely to overshadow their other relationships and needs. Recognizing their individuality beyond being the parent of a child who has autism can bring balance and sanity to this challenging situation.

Autism can be all consuming and is often overwhelming. Recognize that few parents can walk away unscathed. At one extreme, parents can become distraught, even depressed and disconnected, which is a danger in itself. An unavailable parent is the last thing a child with autism needs. Far more common are parents who become, at least initially, preoccupied with or consumed by the child, to the point that they think and talk only about their child or autism. At this point, they may be unable to have a conversation without directing that conversation back to the child or autism. Avoid judging your brother or sister at this stage in their experience with your niece or nephew's autism. Observe what is happening and recognize what they are going through. Let them know you are available and there to help either, directly or indirectly.

Relationships that exist between adult siblings can vary from being loving and supportive to overly sensitive to problematic. Classic "love-hate" situations can often develop rapidly, causing fluctuating emotional reactions and expectations. Any rivalry, anger, or jealousy that might have originated much earlier in life may still be present or may resurface in the face of these new challenges presented by a beloved niece or nephew with autism.

You and your adult brothers or sisters are unique individuals, characterized by your own temperaments, sense of humor, inspirations, beliefs, communication styles, strengths, and weaknesses. Your unique combinations of characteristics, paired with your personal lifestyles and motivations, make you very different individuals while your sibling bonds help you share similarities and first-hand knowledge of one another's strengths and weaknesses. Such a level of intimacy creates potentially more sensitive emotional relationships that need to be handled with care in order to provide support and caring for your adult sibling when he or she is most needed.

It is important to remember that crises humans experience can often be resolved if loved ones have a strong intention to go forward with love and care to fight yet another day. This crisis your sister or brother is experiencing (and in some cases you as well!) is an enormous challenge. Your support and caring are needed and wanted. By participating actively and positively in the process, you can help facilitate a positive resolution to this crisis. You have probably recognized it's all going to take a village to raise a child with special needs. Here is an opportunity for you to serve as a powerful resource for your sibling. There might be some surprising benefits along the way. When you decide you are ready to help, dive right in—there is a lot you can do!

Respect your sibling. Remember that competitiveness from your youth might color your suggestions, and despite your best intentions, you may appear to be critical or patronizing. Be kind and compassionate. No matter how deeply you are grieving over your niece or nephew's autism, you will not begin to feel the intense level of grief your sibling is experiencing. You never really know exactly what he or she is going through.

Recognize that children with autism learn differently. The parenting style that comes so easily with typically developing children and the types described in child-care manuals simply don't apply to children with autism. That is why your brother or sister may become so involved with a wide variety of therapists and agencies, including Applied Behavior Analysis (ABA) therapy and Board Certified Behavior Analysts (BCBAs). Your family members need to learn how to teach and interact with the child (your favorite niece or nephew), so the child learns how to communicate, be socially successful, engage in acceptable behavior, perform well at school, independently complete activities of daily living, and enjoy life.

A simple fun trip into the community.

"I finally had an opportunity to help my sister by taking my nephew, who has autism, on a simple afternoon outing into the community. My plan was to let my sister have some relaxing time alone, to get to know my nephew better and, most importantly, to have some fun with him. My sister gave me a long list of instructions. That set my mind racing. Okay, okay, I can handle taking a little boy out to the mall for a snack. Why doesn't she trust me? It can't be as difficult as she makes it seem. I hope this outing goes well. I am just a little nervous about this, especially since she seems so worried about all these things that could go wrong. But I'm a responsible adult. How bad can it get?

My sister tells me my nephew has sensory issues. She says he will cry and refuse to move if I put the wrong clothes on him, if a tag bothers his neck, if his socks don't line up just perfectly. She tells me that certain sounds will upset him, and he screams with terror if he hears unexpected street noises like sirens or loud honking. He is hard to please with food choices. He prefers only certain brands, and foods have to look a certain way and be a certain color and texture. Crowds of people can be overwhelming for him. Going to the supermarket can be an ordeal, as can the circus, a show with his favorite characters, or his favorite hamburger restaurant. I've heard how he cries constantly at children's shows, ruining it for everyone and having to leave with his mother.

Can this really be true? Maybe my sister is doing something wrong. I am a great aunt, and my nephew and I are in for some fun. Screaming and crying when we are doing what he wants to do? Really? Not on my watch!

First, we go to the grocery store to buy some of his favorite snacks. My nephew suddenly breaks away from me and starts running up an aisle, quickly touching everything he sees. Some items fall. Other people are staring at us and making comments. 'What a terrible mother,' they must be thinking. "What a badly behaved child."

I think he must be hungry; he needs a snack. What did your mother say about the diet? He has temper tantrums if the chicken nuggets are not shaped just right or lined up a certain way. Wait, your mom said when you are hungry you get upset, so you have to eat something. I will get you anything you want to eat. Please just eat something so things don't get worse. Your mom says it's hard, but how hard can it be to get a kid to eat his favorite foods? Suddenly I realize what my sister goes through.

I try to talk to him. He won't look at me or pay any attention to me. It is as if I am not even here with him. Does he even want to be here with me? Does he even like me? I'm being ridiculous. Of course he likes me. Maybe I'm just not doing things right.

Oh no, I think he must have messed on himself! Time for the bathroom! Now I'm taking my six-year- old nephew into the women's restroom with a weak smile on my face as I nod at the staring eyes of others. I need to focus and take care of him, I can do this. Now it's time for me to change a diaper on a rather large, uncooperative six-year-old boy – last time I did this he was six months old.

How am I supposed to do this for an entire afternoon?

After an afternoon like this, you realize what your sister has been experiencing every time she tries to take her child on a fun outing. She is not exaggerating. She does not have poor parenting skills. Day in and day out, she faces the impact autism has on her beloved child. Just like any parent, she wants her child to have fun doing things he enjoys. But she knows the reality that her child often cannot tolerate the surrounding conditions that accompany such experiences. Educate yourself about autism; read and ask questions. Educate yourself about your own niece or nephew. Most children with autism enjoy going out to do some of their favorite activities. However, the sights, smells, noises, people, and activities they experience on such outings may be very difficult to tolerate, thus leading to challenging behaviors. Be sure to be aware; plan, and be prepared in advance. Provide supports to help your niece or nephew tolerate conditions surrounding the experiences he or she enjoys.

Refer to **Activity C** in the Appendix for some great ideas on creating an autism care kit.

Also refer to **Activity H** for Tips on eating and toileting.

Remember that children with autism often like attention, warm affection, and enjoy the company of others. However, their response to typical social situations and overtures might be very atypical and can make you incorrectly conclude they do not enjoy social attention.

Remember, any behavior, no matter how aberrant it might seem, usually communicates something about what that child needs. The challenge is to recognize what the child is trying to communicate, acknowledge that communication, and address the underlying need the behavior is expressing. Never assume their poor behaviors might be because of bad parenting. Such assumptions are unfair and damaging to both the child who has autism and to the parents. Be compassionate and understanding. Ask if you can do something to help, but do not be surprised if your adult sibling says he or she just needs some time alone or wants a different focus for a while. Wait for the crisis behavior to pass and then ask your sibling what causes the child to engage in that behavior, what you can do to help prevent it from occurring, what you can do to calm the child, and what your sibling can do to help you learn about the child's needs.

Many children with autism seem to be in a world of their own and show no interest in responding to greetings or waving goodbye when you leave, but do not assume they are not interested in connecting with you. Do assume they may have difficulty learning what those responses might be or tolerating the sights, smells, sounds, or unpredictable details involved in such tasks that we take for granted every day.

CASE EXAMPLE

Aunt Melissa loved her nephew, Casey, who has autism, but she was not physically able to manage his aggressive outbursts. She wanted to provide support for her brother and sister-in-law who were Casey's parents, but could not watch Casey on her own. One day while Aunt Melissa was with Casey, his mother, and his sister, Bella, at the mall, he had a meltdown. They had to leave the mall and go home early. Bella commented in a resentful voice, "That's not fair. I finally get to go to the mall and Casey ruins it. I hate autism!" Aunt Melissa realized that Bella had gotten "lost" in all the efforts being made to help Casey. Bella's needs were being overlooked. She discovered a way to help! She made a "mall date" with Bella for the next weekend. They enjoyed some quality time together and Bella stopped feeling Casey's behavior determined all of her experiences and activities. Bella and Aunt Melissa scheduled fun activities regularly after that. Having one less person in the house when Bella was out with Aunt Melissa also gave Casey and his mother some quieter time with fewer people talking and being active, so Casey could relax and Mom could focus on activities at home without Bella interrupting or complaining.

An aunt and uncle can:

- Become educated. Education is a powerful therapeutic tool. Read, go to conferences, attend support groups (ask permission first, of course).
- Perhaps you can attend a doctor's office visit.
- Learn the intervention program. Find out what Applied Behavioral Analysis Therapy (ABA) is and what a BCBA actually does. Learn the techniques and incorporate them into the repertoire of responses you have in interacting with your niece or nephew.
- Ask your sister or brother if you can:
  o Run an errand;
  o Help on community outings to ease the difficulty of supervising the child while also completing errands or activities;
  o Do the laundry;
  o Help repair something;
  o Babysit for an hour, for an evening, or maybe overnight;
  o Cook a meal;
  o Spend the night so your sibling can get a night's sleep;
  o Provide additional love, support, and fun for the child's brothers and sisters who may feel left out or neglected.
- Consider yourself a Team Member.

CASE EXAMPLE

Uncle Clark loved his nephew, Will, who had autism. He usually took Will to buy toys and treats while Will's mom took a nap (if Will had kept her up the night before) or took care of chores around the house that were too difficult to handle when Will was home. But Uncle Clark could not get Will to engage with him when they were at Will's house. When they were at the store or a fast food restaurant, Will told Uncle Clark what he wanted and Uncle Clark bought it and gave it to him. One day Uncle Clark came to the house to get Will. Will excitedly yelled the name of a toy he wanted. Uncle Clark thought Will was simply associating him with getting toys and treats, rather than actually having a social relationship with him. A few days later Uncle Clark asked Will's mom if he could go with her to some of Will's therapy sessions so maybe he could learn other ways to bond with Will. Will's therapist showed Uncle Clark how to prompt Will to interact with him socially. She included Uncle Clark in some of Will's play and leisure activities during his therapy sessions. Uncle Clark was able to see Will at home and play with him, instead of only taking him to buy treats and toys. One day, several months later, Uncle Clark arrived at the house, Will saw him and yelled "Uncle Clark! Uncle Clark!" Uncle Clark was overjoyed.

CHAPTER 8

Close Friends

F riends of a parent often take the place of extended biological family members, or indeed can become extended family members. Traditional roles do not always apply in such situations, so be flexible and incorporate friendships in ways that work best for everyone involved. For example, if one set of grandparents does not live nearby, or if friction exists, closeness might develop with your best friend's parents. "Adoptive" grandparents can provide a special relationship for both you and your child. In some instances, trusted neighbors may assume the role of aunts and uncles. Appreciate their love and support for you, your child, and your family. If you are a close friend of someone who has a child with autism, you may be in a position to help in unique ways.

Ask your friend what is needed. Of course, your friend may be so entrenched in meeting the needs of her child and family each day, she may not be able to view the situation and needs from a broader perspective, in the same way as a friend who is on the outside looking in.

Close friends can help in unique ways. Consider helping by:
- Researching information for your friend.
- Encouraging and planning/preparing stress-management activities for your friend.
- Advocating for your friend's child, with her permission.
- Helping set up diets or finding simple meals plans or recipes that support the child's special diet.
- Locating professionals who may be of service, including babysitters, life planners, financial planners, legal advisers, advocates, medical professionals, specialists, therapists, etc.
- Scheduling meetings with your friend's permission.
- Attending meetings and appointments to provide support for your friend and to take notes.
- Using your own areas of expertise to help your friend, such as addressing guardianship issues, insurance needs, home improvements, shopping, food planning, and preparation.
- Call more often.
- Stay for coffee and a long visit, even if you do household tasks together while visiting.
- Listen without judging.
- Continue to extend invitations.

Friendships can be very fragile, especially when one or both friends are experiencing challenges. It is easy to be a friend when times are good. When confronted by challenging times, our real friends try to stand by us. Support your friend and your friend's family after a diagnosis of autism. Accept the child for who he/she is and help the child in any way possible. One of the greatest gifts you can give a friend affected by autism is to support his/her family. Being a friend who listens and offers understanding, even when you don't understand, is a most challenging task, yet it is one of the most rewarding gifts you can offer a friend.

Miscellaneous gifts some people have given to a friend who has a child with autism include:

- Providing access to information or legal expertise related to guardianship issues or life-planning issues.
- Setting up a special needs trust or helping solicit funding for therapy.
- Helping your friend navigate the often frustrating maze of insurance to cover the cost of therapy.
- Helping with car-pooling or transportation to the doctor.
- Using your knowledge of nutrition and planning or preparing special diets.
- Scheduling monthly meetings with the child's team to discuss progress, areas of concern, and planning.
- Providing educational advocacy for school-aged children.
- Simply being there with your friend during meetings with the school or therapists. A friendly face around the table can provide much needed support.
- Learning the educational rules related to autism and school services.
- Communicating with schools, writing letters, scheduling appointments.
- Knowing about the school curriculum.

- Knowing about different therapies such as ABA (Applied Behavior Analysis), OT (Occupational Therapy), speech therapy, etc.
- Recording the meetings.
- Taking notes.
- Writing follow-up letters confirming action items.
- Confirming upcoming appointments.

Learn to recognize when your friend is stressed. Some parents try to act strong so they are not perceived as being incompetent or weak. How can you help your friend at these times? Help identify barriers to obtaining help. Are the barriers financial, a lack of motivation, denial, exhaustion, confusion, feeling overwhelmed, or something else? Your knowledge of what your friend is going through at these times can help ease his/her burden.

Encourage your friend to practice stress management! Refer to **Activity E**.

Single parents and extended family members

For single parents, parent friendships might take the place of spouses and/ or extended biological family members. "Adoptive" aunts, uncles, or grandparents can be wonderful sources of support. There are so many aspects to raising a child with autism, and any assistance is likely to be welcome. You can offer activities such as babysitting, running errands, doing the laundry, Internet researches, providing transportation, and a host of other supports.

Parents, especially single parents, often say things like:

- I don't have friends who "get it" and support me or accept me. Ask about your friend first – before asking about the child.
- It's not fair to be told to "make sure you make time for yourself" when I don't have time to do anything differently. Set up fun times!

- Others tell me to get a babysitter. What if no one wants to take care of a child who behaves aggressively? Offer to babysit or to go over to visit. Local university or college programs may have students with some training in autism, who are willing to babysit. Contact local schools and inquire about trained child-care providers. They may even have some paraprofessionals or teachers trained and experienced with autism who want to earn extra money outside of school hours. Leave your contact information for them.
- I feel overwhelmed with all the things I need to do! Let them know you are there for them and that you are a good listener!

 CAUTION

- Avoid telling your friend to de-stress or take care of himself or herself. Instead, plan or provide a stress-relieving activity.
- Don't worry about bothering your friend by calling or stopping by to visit. Call and talk, listen, and there for your friend.
- Avoid offering advice when your friend complains or you see a problem occur. Ask and show concern. Give advice only if asked.

CHAPTER 9

Cousins

O ur cousins come in all sizes and from all age groups. They may be infants, toddlers, school age adolescents, and/or adults. Cousins have a unique relationship with one another. They are closer to the social situations in which children find themselves during most of their school days; however, they do not have the same daily closeness or rivalries siblings, step-siblings, or classmates experience among one another. Some children who do not have siblings may establish surrogate relationships with one or more of their cousins when they have opportunities to socialize in a relaxed, comfortable setting with access to shared interests. Many children with autism learn best when they are exposed to typical peers who model language, social skills, self-care, and other prosocial behaviors.

Cousins are uniquely placed to provide friendship, a good example, coherent explanations, and companionship for their cousins with autism, without the overfamiliarity, jealousy, rigid expectations, or rivalries that often accompany relationships with siblings. To better understand what we can do to help cousins develop meaningful relationships with their loved ones who have autism, let's start by exploring the different levels of social interest your child may have in other people. Social interest is often unrelated to the person's age or functioning level. Some children who are nonverbal and dependent on others for completing even the simplest daily living tasks may be more socially interested than the young adult who has Asperger's syndrome, talks fluently, and is highly intelligent. On the other hand, many individuals across the autism spectrum demonstrate social interest but do not have the social skills or tolerance needed to develop or maintain reciprocal relationships with peers.

Socially unaware or disinterested

Some children with autism have not developed awareness of their peers. They may play in the same vicinity, but do not display any interest in joining peers for play. They may interact with peers to obtain access to toys or other preferred items, but not for the purpose of sharing an activity.

Be careful to end this "playdate" before the cousin with autism becomes overwhelmed and tries to escape or has a meltdown.

Extended family members can facilitate social growth in a cousin who has autism and who is socially unaware or disinterested by helping him or her to:

- Be in the same play area for tolerable amounts of time.

- Provide duplicate high-preference toys *at this point in the child's growth*, to avoid fighting over toys, which can negatively affect future play dates.

- Talk aloud about what the children are doing periodically throughout the play date. Provide "no adult talking" breaks in between narrations to prevent over-stimulation and compromised self-regulation.

- Involve the child's ABA therapist in play dates or talk to the therapist about bringing one of the cousins to a therapy session so they can practice playing near one another with therapeutic guidance. The ABA therapist can help the child learn to tolerate having a peer playing nearby and eventually facilitate social interaction.

CASE EXAMPLE

Rose is four years old and she has autism. When Rose's cousin, Marie, came over with her mother, Rose ignored Marie. She did not look at Marie or speak to her. However, when Marie picked up one of Rose's favorite dolls, Rose screamed, grabbed the doll and shoved Marie to the floor. Marie screamed and cried. Marie's mother comforted her and they found a doll that Marie brought from home so she could play with a doll, too. Then Rose's mother began imitating something she had seen Rose's ABA therapist do during some of Rose's therapy sessions. She began narrating short scripts related to what Rose and Marie were doing with their dolls. When Marie picked up her doll and picked up a bottle to feed her, Rose's mom quietly said "Oh, my baby is hungry. I can give her a bottle of milk to drink. She likes that." Then Rose grabbed for the bottle and her mom said, "Your baby is hungry too. She can have the bottle next. Wai-ai-ai-t." When Marie had paused after giving her doll the bottle, Rose's mom said, "Rose's turn. Rose's baby is hungry too. Rose needs to feed her baby now. Thank you!" Then she gave the bottle to Rose to feed her baby. After several weeks of repeating this script, Rose approached Marie and gave her the bottle to give to her baby. This was the first step in showing social awareness and interest. Over time with such guidance from their moms, Rose and Marie began interacting more and more during their playdates.

Socially aware or interested, but unable to tolerate many social situations

Some children with autism are aware of, and interested in, playing with peers, but have difficulty tolerating what happens within a social situation such as the length of playtime, the number of other children, sharing, excessive talking, over-stimulating activities, or playing with toys/engaging in activities that are not highly preferred. These children yearn for playmates, but often engage in behaviors that offend, confuse, frighten, or hurt peers when they are unable to tolerate some aspects of a play situation. The adults can take steps to ensure successful play dates by being aware of their child's tolerance limits and planning play dates so the child will not be overwhelmed.

Involved adults can help cousins learn to play together by:
- managing playtime by incorporating breaks so children can tolerate the length of time spent playing together or being in the same area together;
- limiting the number of children and adults in the same area;
- limiting the amount of "background" stimulation, such as adults visiting too loudly or too emotionally, background noises, strong smells from food or other items, distracting objects that are off limits, or open access to "off-limits" areas or activities;
- providing duplicate high-preference toys until the children have learned to share, recognizing that sharing will need to be directly taught and practiced;
- providing interesting activities and toys.

CASE EXAMPLE

Kaleah loved playing with her mermaids. Her parents tried to join in her play, but Kaleah moved away from them. Her brothers did not want to play mermaids with Kaleah. Her Aunt Nina suggested that her daughter, Missy, could come over to play mermaids with Kaleah, who was three years older than Missy. Missy loved mermaids too. When Missy came over, she and Kaleah would run through the house squealing and chasing each other and tumbling on the floor together. Eventually, their moms insisted they remain in the playroom, and put up a gate to prevent them from running through the house. The first few playdates ended with Kaleah having a screaming meltdown after 30 minutes playing with the mermaids. Kaleah's mom realized she was overly excited and could not tolerate longer than 30 minutes of social interaction, so they set a timer for 25 minutes. When the timer chimed, one of the moms said, "time for a break," which meant the girls could still have some mermaids to play with, but they played in separate areas of the house for 20 minutes. When the timer chimed after 25 minutes, they could play together in the same area again. As Kaleah was able to play without meltdowns, they lengthened the playtime by a few minutes each week until she was able to play for longer periods without a break. Eventually, they were able to play together, taking breaks on their own as they needed to without a timed break. Their moms also gradually introduced other toys into their playdates.

CASE EXAMPLE

Uncle Luis and Aunt Lisa had two sons who were younger than their cousin with autism, Miguel. Although Miguel wanted friends, he did not have any his age, and his interests aligned with those of much younger children. One day Aunt Lisa and Miguel's mother were visiting and talking about their children. They realized their three children enjoyed playing in the park and on the playground equipment at the park. They had not considered having the boys play together since their ages were so different. They made a playdate and met at the park. Miguel played with his cousins, and all three boys had a fun time. Miguel's mother was so excited to have found some playmates for Miguel. They began meeting regularly at the park, and on rainy days they met at Miguel or Aunt Lisa's house. The boys discovered other activities they enjoyed doing together. Miguel's mother taught them what Miguel acted like when he needed a quiet break away from talking, people, and playing. They learned what to do and say when Miguel needed those breaks. After taking a break, Miguel would rejoin the fun on his own. He was happy to have his cousins as his friends, too.

Socially aware or interested, but does not have the skills needed to develop and maintain relationships with peers.

When a child has demonstrated social awareness and/or interest, but does not have the skills needed to develop and maintain meaningful relationships with peers, the required social skills usually must be directly taught and practiced. These are the situations in which interventions such as *Social Stories*® by Carol Gray, *Comic Strip Conversations*® by Carol Gray, acting and theater classes, video modeling and other direct instruction and rehearsal methods, along with direct instruction and feedback regarding interactions with peers, are beneficial. At this level of social functioning, nothing is more important to the child with autism than a reliable social partner who likely is not a sibling and does not share a home with them. The perfect role for a cousin! If the child who has autism gravitates to younger peers, then a younger cousin may be a better match at this point in time, than a same-age or older cousin.

Facilitate play between cousins at this level by:
- Directly teaching and practicing the steps to the social skills needed to have a successful play date.
- Viewing and discussing videos of children interacting.
- Discussing what the child wants to learn related to playing with his or her cousin.
- Incorporating new or different toys or "props" into play sessions.
- Assigning skills for the child to use when playing with his or her cousin.

CASE EXAMPLE

Martin wanted friends. He invited his cousin, Joel, over to play since they both enjoyed playing video games and Wii. When Joel arrived, Martin was the perfect host. He greeted Joel and invited him in. Then Martin offered Joel a snack and a drink, prepared them, and brought them to Joel. Then he asked Joel what he wanted to play. Martin made sure Joel had everything he needed to be comfortable and to have fun. Then Martin left and watched TV in the living room while Joel played video games in Martin's bedroom by himself. Martin knew how to be a great host, but he did not know what to do and say to actually play with Joel. Martin's mother spoke to his ABA therapist about this and asked her to teach Martin how to play with his cousin. The therapist taught Martin what to do and say when his cousin came to visit. They wrote a script for the playdates, rehearsed, made a video of a "final rehearsal," then reviewed the video and rehearsed parts of the script that needed "polishing." Once Martin had learned a script for his playdates, they were able to incorporate flexibility into the scripts, so he learned a more natural play interaction to use.

 CAUTION

Avoid teaching too many social skills at one time. Prioritize by teaching the skills that are critical for the cousin to return for a follow-up playdate, before focusing on skills that are niceties. Also be sure to teach the child behaviors that help him fit in with his peers, as opposed to adult-pleasing behaviors that may cause him to look very different from peers or to be ostracized by peers.

Socially aware of peers, but disinterested in developing or maintaining relationships with peers

Some children who have autism are socially aware of peers, but have no interest in developing or maintaining relationships with them or any other children. These children often prefer the company of adults, especially adults who share an area of keen interest with them. These children still need to learn and rehearse social skills, but will likely not obtain social satisfaction from playdates with cousins who are not adults. If they have cousins or other relatives who are adults and who share similar interests in one or more areas, then developing those relationships will likely be beneficial.

Cousins of children who prefer adult company can help by:
- inviting the child to events, even if they anticipate the child will not want to participate;
- including the child in activities he or she is interested in;
- sharing common interests;
- continuing to greet the child and speaking to him or her, even if you do not receive a response;
- continuing to be kind and to interact with the child in a friendly manner;
- learning about the child's individual needs and skills in order to better understand what he or she can tolerate and do.

CASE EXAMPLE

Spence has autism. He was very interested in dinosaurs. His older cousin, Martin, was a science teacher who shared Spence's love of prehistoric creatures. He showed Spence books, pictures, and videos of dinosaurs. However, Martin realized Spence's fixation on dinosaurs was quite extreme and too limited. He also realized Spence did not tolerate new information being introduced. So, instead of trying to introduce new topics to Spence, Martin decided to simply expand on what Spence already loved, so he expanded his interests without Spence being upset or resisting new information. Martin explained to Spence that fossils were the bones of dinosaurs. Spence was fascinated and soon began reading, looking at, and watching whatever he could about fossils. He and Martin started a fossil collection. Then Martin expanded on this broadened topic by teaching Spence about volcanoes and rocks from prehistoric times. They enjoyed reading and looking at all the information they could find about volcanoes and rocks. Martin enjoyed these visits as much as Spence did. Martin gradually expanded Spence's interests again by introducing other aspects of science, as it was related to the information Spence had already learned about. Although Spence avoided peers, Martin was even able to include another cousin with similar interests in some of their visits. Spence willingly interacted with his other cousin so they could talk about their favorite topics.

Cousins are in a one-of-a-kind role to model appropriate behaviors and to provide unique social opportunities for their cousins who have autism. Cousins who have grown up with children with autism or who have spent significant time with them from a younger age may not need a great amount of training regarding autism as it affects their cousin. Spending a significant amount of time together under adult supervision that promotes caring, respectful interactions starting at younger ages will allow cousins to learn about one another's individual likes, dislikes, tolerance levels, and interaction styles through observation, shared experiences, direct teaching, and guidance. Supervising adults can teach peer sensitization and support by promoting tolerance and social understanding. This can be facilitated by teaching and motivating respect for tolerance levels by prompting breaks when the adults observe one or more of the cousins may have reached their tolerance limit, so the children do not resort to aggression, tantrums, or meltdowns out of frustration or anxiety. Social understanding can be facilitated by saying aloud what a cousin may be trying to communicate or may be thinking, so the other cousins understand and can then respond more effectively. Cousins can provide peer modeling of language and behavior with the support of supervising adults by demonstrating language, actions, play behaviors, social skills, and self-care skills, and encourage a cousin who has autism to imitate those behaviors. Adults can teach cousins how to obtain the other child's attention before demonstrating a skill. Ideally, these teaching opportunities need to be approached casually and should not consist of the cousins trying to imitate a therapy session. The most important factor is for the cousins to have a fun shared experience in whatever way works best for all of them.

CHAPTER 10

Surviving and Enjoying Special Events and Holidays

Holidays and special events are a very important part of family life. They present opportunities for families and extended families to share traditions, activities, time together, and memories. Holidays can be fun, but overwhelming. Parents of children who have autism often find such events very stressful, and many families avoid attending these events. Others may have one parent or a caretaker remain at home with the child with autism to avoid exposing him or her to stressful events or to avoid exposing others to their child's unusual behavior. Some children with autism may refuse to attend or participate in activities related to holidays and special events.

Holidays and special events can be overwhelming. What seems fun to some children may be very stressful to a child who has autism. Rather than avoiding participating in special events and holiday traditions, anticipate what challenges may occur, plan ahead, prepare yourself, your family and your child, and enjoy!

Holidays and special events to plan and prepare for include:

- Restaurants
- Church
- Birthdays and birthday parties
- Sporting events
- Community events
- School events
- Movies
- Swimming
- Zoo trips
- Reunions
- Weddings
- Funerals
- Holiday gatherings
- Unplanned or unexpected events
- Vacations
- Short visits
- Extended visits
- Family members moving in or moving away
- Living with extended family
- Babysitters

Ten steps for enjoying holidays and special events

1. Keep it simple.

   - Don't overdo it;
   - Don't expect or try to have the "perfect" holiday or event;
   - Select experiences that are fun for your child without being overwhelming;
   - Know what your child can tolerate and respect his or her tolerance limits within the activity you are attending.

 CASE EXAMPLE

Nathan's mother loves to decorate and cook. She wanted to have all the family's aunts, uncles, grandparents, and cousins over for Thanksgiving dinner. While Nathan was at school one day, she put up decorations all around the house. When Nathan came home, he was very agitated and began pulling down the decorations. His mother realized she had changed Nathan's environment, which upset and confused him, so she took the decorations down. Once Nathan had calmed down, she had him choose a decoration and watch her display it. She only decorated the dining room, and then waited two or three days to decorate the living room. She limited the number of decorations she used so Nathan could enjoy the holiday also. Nathan was able to tolerate these gradual changes he observed taking place.

---

2. Be prepared.

   - Bring a survival pack that may include some or all of the following:
     - Printed or picture schedule
     - Visual cues

- High protein snacks
- Drinks
- Supports for surviving public restrooms, such as preferred toilet paper, wet wipes, sticky paper, or duct tape to cover toilet and hand dryer sensors, preferred soap, a preferred hand towel, etc.
- Timer
- Transition object
- Comfort items such as a hat, blanket, iPad, or other preferred electronics, favorite toys, etc.
- Quiet, calming activities and items
- Supports individualized for your child's needs such as noise cancelling headphones, chewy toys, music, books, art activities, etc.
- A change of clothing, especially if your child is expected to wear dress-up clothes or a special outfit during an event
- Any other items that help your child stay calm and maintain self-control

CASE EXAMPLE

Jacques was 15 years old. He was very smart and talkative. He had meltdowns in the car when his grandmother ran errands on Saturday mornings; however, Jacques' mother was working and it was not safe for him to stay home alone. Jacques would stall while getting dressed to run errands. His grandmother would set a time at which they would leave. Oftentimes, Jacques had been slow dressing, so he did not eat breakfast before they left the house. Once in the car, Jacques would demand that his grandmother stop at a fast-food restaurant because he was hungry. He would have a meltdown and become aggressive when she refused to stop. Jacques' grandmother finally realized Jacques probably would not learn to dress faster so he could eat breakfast before leaving the house, so she created a routine in which Jacques put items from a checklist into his backpack, which he carried to the car. The items included high-protein snacks and a drink. Jacques ate the items on the way to the store, before he began demanding to stop at a fast-food restaurant. Jacques stopped having meltdowns or acting aggressively toward his grandmother during errands since he was able to eat something substantial.

3. Have a plan for:
   - Safety;
   - Helping your child feel secure;
   - Restroom breaks;
   - Meals/snacks;
   - Graceful exit when your child shows early warning signs (don't wait until he or she is out of control!);

- What to say and do if your child displays inappropriate behavior that imposes on others;
- Meltdowns.

 CASE EXAMPLE

During a family reunion at a big restaurant, Maya started getting out of her seat and squealing loudly. She had finished eating. Some others were eating, but most had finished eating and were talking loudly and laughing. Maya's mother was visiting and had not noticed the change in Maya's behavior. Maya's aunt noticed and she got Maya's favorite toy out of the bag in which she carried her special items. She also retrieved Maya's "break" picture and showed it to Maya along with her toy. She whispered, "I've got this" to Maya's mother as they went to a bench in another part of the restaurant where it was quieter. She let Maya play with her toy until Maya had calmed down, was able to sit for several minutes, and was not squealing. Once Maya was calm for several minutes, they returned to the reunion and Maya was able to sit quietly and play with her toy.

---

4. Provide supports for your child using one or more of the following:
   - Physical supports such as preplanned movement activities, quiet breaks from stimulation, visuals to cue your child to take a break or that your child can use to request a break;
   - Visual supports such as picture cues, checklists, picture schedules, picture task sequences such as the steps for using the toilet, "first _____, then _____" strips, token reward systems, event calendars, etc.;
   - Transition objects;

- Embed familiar rituals within the events of the holiday or special activity;
- Provide a relaxation activity before and after difficult activities.

 CASE EXAMPLE

Carlos' father and stepmother had a birthday party for his stepbrother, Jace. When it was time to open the presents, Carlos grabbed the present his stepmother was handing to Jace. His father said sternly, "No Carlos, not yours," and Carlos started to grab all the presents and screamed. His stepmother remembered a ritual through which they used to teach Carlos to share. She said "Carlos, it is Jace's turn." Carlos stopped grabbing the presents and let Jace open them.

---

5. Help your child understand and practice the plan in advance by doing one or more of the following:
   - Prepare and read stories that teach about the event;
   - Rehearse; some children may need to rehearse and practice for several weeks in advance of the event;
   - Provide visuals of the plan;
   - Upon arrival at the setting where the activity will occur, take your child and show him or her where to go to take a break and practice, so using the area will become familiar and more comfortable before it is needed.

CASE EXAMPLE

Grannie took Neisha to the mall to buy a Father's Day present for her dad. Neisha is easily overwhelmed, so as soon as they arrived at the mall, Grannie took her to look at the restroom before she needed to use it. She also found a bench in a quiet area of the mall, and they sat for a few minutes before starting to shop. Grannie knew Neisha would be able to relax in the restroom and on the bench once she was familiar with their location and what it looked and felt like, before she needed to use them.

6. Respect your child's tolerance limits for:
   - Decorations;
     - How they look
     - How they sound
     - How they smell
     - How they feel
   - Costumes, props, dress-up clothes, or other special outfits;
     - How they feel
     - How they sound
     - How they smell
     - How they look
     - How long they have to be worn
   - Activities;
     - How noisy and how much talking your child is exposed to
     - How many people and how close to other people
     - What types of movement the child and others will be displaying
     - How complicated
     - How interesting it is to your child

- How competitive
- Your child may need to watch the activity first
- Social gatherings;
  - How many people
  - How familiar are the people to your child
  - How and when will others approach, touch, or talk to your child
  - How noisy
  - What types of smells
  - Politely ignore or explain what your child needs them to do when it is apparent they do not understand your child's needs, interests, and limits.
  - Remember, you know your child best!

 CASE EXAMPLE

Tracy's stepson, Jeremy, was nine years old. Jeremy often had meltdowns when they went grocery shopping, but Tracy had to get groceries on the weekends when she was home from work and there was no one who could watch Jeremy for her. She had become tired of the stares and comments when Jeremy had a meltdown, but knew it would not help to express her feelings. One day Tracy typed a short paragraph that filled half a sheet of paper. It explained what autism is, what causes meltdowns, and what to do or say when someone witnesses a meltdown. She made several copies and now carries them with her when she is in public with Jeremy. When someone stares or comments, Tracy simply smiles politely and hands them a copy of the information.

7. Know when to stop.

- Recognize and respect your child's early warning signs that indicate he or she is having difficulty tolerating or managing a situation.

- Have a preplanned exit strategy; teach and rehearse this exit strategy with your child in advance.

- If your child has frequent severe meltdowns from which he or she is unable to recover quickly or is at high risk of such a meltdown during this particular situation, and there is no quiet place you can take him or her to regain self-control, consider taking two vehicles to the event. Ideally, be prepared to leave before your child actually has a meltdown. Allow your child to indicate when he or she needs a break or wants to sit in the car or leave after being engaged in the activity for a set amount of time.

 CASE EXAMPLE

Nelson took his stepson, Tony, to meet a friend for a playdate at the park. After playing near each other for 10 minutes, Tony started moving away from his friend and was squealing loudly. Nelson realized Tony was becoming agitated, so he got Tony's transition object and took him to a bench where he could regain self-control. Tony continued to have problems, so Nelson told the other parent, "I think we are at our limit for today. See you next time." He then took Tony home before any further problems occurred that could have a negative impact on his relationship on future play dates.

8. Have realistic expectations. Remember, they:
   - may not be your original expectations;
   - may be different than expectations for other children;
   - may need to be adjusted as needed.

 CASE EXAMPLE

Miguel was very excited about Halloween. His grandmother had taken him to the store and they had found a costume he liked. Every day he asked when he could wear his costume for Halloween and trick or treat. When Halloween evening arrived, Miguel put on his costume. However, when he saw it was dark outside and noticed the Halloween decorations in the neighbors' yards, Miguel ran back into the house and refused to go back outside. He wanted to go trick or treating but was too afraid. His father tried to reason with him, but Miguel would not change his mind. Miguel began to have a meltdown. His grandmother, who lived with Miguel and his family, took Miguel's hand and led him over to the sofa where they sat down. She said in a soft voice, "I need someone to help me with trick or treaters. Will you help me? They would like to see your costume, and you can give them treats, not tricks." Miguel spent that Halloween passing out treats and wearing his costume. He had a great time for Halloween, although it was not what they had originally planned.

---

9. Plan alternatives.
   - Create your own traditions that help your child have fun.
   - You may need alternative activities, instead of the activities originally planned.
   - You may need alternative activities imbedded within ongoing activities.

CASE EXAMPLE

All of Jena's girl siblings and cousins were gathering at Aunt Josie's house for a slumber party. Aunt Josie wanted Jena to enjoy the slumber party too. Jena joined the other girls for dancing and music, making s'mores (Jena made her own version because she does not like marshmallows), and jumping on the bed. When it was time for activities that involved a lot of talking and giggling, Jena was not interested, so Aunt Josie had an alternate activity for Jena. She enjoyed playing with some stuffed animals in another part of the house away from all the talking and giggling. When the other girls wanted to stay up all night, Aunt Josie invited Jen to bring her sleeping bag into the spare bedroom to sleep. Jena spent time with her friends and was included in the slumber party. She was also allowed to engage in activities that were fun for her and leave the group when she wanted to.

10. Enjoy the present moment.
- Take care of yourself
  - Get enough sleep
  - Get adequate nutrition
  - Don't overdo it
  - Take some time for yourself and plan some "adult time"
  - Treat yourself to something special
- Feel comfortable saying "no" to events that don't work for your whole family.
- Feel comfortable scheduling your child to stay with a trusted caretaker during events your child is unable to tolerate.
- Accept help when offered.

- Trade child-free time with another trusted parent within brief time frames.
- Rehearse a scripted response to use when others who do not understand your child are trying to impose their way. For example, smile and say, "Thank you, but we just need some quiet time away from people right now."
- Have fun in ways your child and family will enjoy!

Holiday tips

- Don't overdo it.
- Avoid decorations your child cannot tolerate.
- Prepare your child for seeing decorations in public.
- Allow your child to select and/or display decorations within clear boundaries you set in advance.

Shopping tips

- Go early or during low-volume shopping times.
- When teaching your child to tolerate shopping, start by going to smaller, quieter stores to pick up one item. View this as a training session, with you or with your child's therapist as the trainer/coach, not as a shopping trip to meet any shopping needs. As your child is successful, gradually increase the length of your shopping time or the number of items purchased, and gently introduce your child to busier stores. However, avoid taking your child into noisy, busy stores for lengthy shopping trips. Intersperse your normal shopping outings with short trips and visiting smaller, less stimulating stores.
- Shop while your child is at school or with a caretaker.
- Shop online (it's fun to shop for unique items in your PJs!!!)

Tips for family gatherings

- Politely ignore comparisons, judgments, and well-intentioned re-marks made by people who do not understand your child. Some family members carry information cards about autism to give to people who do not understand.
- Politely ignore relatives and friends who try to tell you how to discipline or treat your child; it's okay to offer to help them learn about your child at a later time.
- Family gatherings are not appropriate occasions to lecture or correct family members about autism. Make a mental note that you need to talk and/or share information in the future with someone who does not understand.
- Trust your own instincts.
- Concentrate on having a good time!

Tips when dressing up

- Select clothing style or costume, fabric, and details your child can tolerate, while still wearing clothing appropriate for the situation.
- Use visual cues and a timer to help your child predict when uncomfortable clothing can be removed and the comfortable outfit you brought in his or her survival pack can be worn.

Tips for helping your child enjoy activities

- Select activities your child prefers or use a "first _____, then _____" visual to show your child that after the activity she or he can engage in a preferred activity.
- Try to make the most of your time together.
- Stop the activity before it becomes overwhelming.

- Forewarn your child before the end of the activity, especially if he or she is enjoying it.
- Provide a visual that shows the next activity.
- Schedule a preferred or interesting activity that will follow an activity your child may resist stopping.
- Alternate high-stimulation activities with low-stimulation activities.
- Alternate activities during which your child is exposed to other people talking, with activities that do not expose him or her to talking.
- Provide activities that offer a physical outlet for energy or aggression.
- Carefully adjust the timing and pacing of activities to meet your child's individual needs.

Tips for changes in routine

- Plan and prepare in advance using visuals and timers, thus making changes predictable.
- Have a scripted phrase such as "uh oh; look" and show your child the sequence of the change and the next event, using pictures or other visuals when unexpected changes occur.
- Create a holiday or special event schedule and calendar.
- Provide increased calming supports to help your child tolerate changes and to help you tolerate changes too!

Don't just survive the holidays and fun special events; ENJOY them in your own, unique way!

CHAPTER 11

Conclusion

Emily Perl Kingsley compared having a child with autism to landing up in Holland when you were planning to travel to Italy. If you spend the rest of your life mourning the fact that you didn't get to see Italy, you may never be free to enjoy the very special, lovely things about Holland. The extended family is a child's strongest social support. With intervention and comprehensive programming, any child's outcome can be improved. With an extended family on a loved one's side, that can only be optimized. Then we can all mindfully see our children against the sky. When we can do that and accept that loved one who is ours, we will be healed.

APPENDIX

Activities

Activity A - Who is your extended family?

Most people are part of a larger family unit that may include grandparents, aunts, uncles, cousins, nieces, and nephews, along with immediate family members. Many families extend far beyond biological connections to form important bonds with others who are a valuable part of their lives, such as close friends. Extended family members may or may not live within the nuclear household.

Many families extend to include:
- Parents and siblings;
- Step-parents and step-siblings;
- In-laws;
- Grandparents, aunts, uncles, cousins, nieces, nephews, and other relatives;
- Partners;
- Close friends.

Who Is In Your Child's Extended Family?

relatives & friends rarely contacted

relatives & friends contacted
occasionally

relatives & close friends living
outside your home

others living in your home

parents & siblings in a
different home / stepfamilies

child, parent(s)
& siblings they
live with

Alex and her mother's extended family circle looks like this.

Alex lives with her mother. She sometimes visits her dad and stepmom.

Jody (Mom's best friend)

Nana & Grampy, Aunt Jen,
Uncle Rocky & cousin Ben

Dad & stepmom Lisa

Alex & Mom

Miguel and his parents' extended family circle look like this.

Miguel lives with his parents and sister Tina.

Mami's cousin Ramon, Papi's friend
Mason and neighbors Roxi & John

Grandma & Grandpa Jones,
Uncle Randy and Mami &
Papi's friends Janet & Mike

Grandma & Grandpa Garcia,
Tia Lisa & several cousins

Miguel, Mami, Papi
& Tina

Hunter and his grandma's extended family circle look like this.

Hunter lives with his grandma.

Grandma's son (Hunter's Uncle
Joe) who lives overseas

Grandma's friend Liz

Hunter & Grandma

Everyone's extended family circle looks different. Family circles may change over time and circumstances. Many family circles consist of biological relatives, stepfamilies, and friends. Some extended families consist mainly of relatives, while others may consist only of friends and others who are not biological relatives.

Extended family members can help a loved one with autism by understanding their own comfort levels and learning how to support the parents and child in their own ways.

Fill in the names of your loved one's extended family

Activity B - Conflict resolution for the extended family.

It is not unusual for family members to have differing views and opinions

If you sense tension between you and your loved one, such as your adult child—own it!

Avoid blaming, scolding, or shaming others for what is happening. Be aware that these types of responses to conflict may have become a pattern that has been ingrained in you since childhood. You are an adult now and can choose how you will respond to conflict. You are not destined to respond based on what you experienced as a child.

- For example, have the awareness and courage to recognize that you might not relate well to your grandchild/nephew/cousin/friend's child because of
  - their disability
  - their behavior
  - or because you disagree with the treatment methods used
- Avoid feeling guilty, unwanted, or disrespected because you are no longer in charge. This could be your finest hour, but only if you have the courage and wisdom to learn from what is happening.
- Recognize that you are likely to feel overwhelmed and unsure of what to do and how to act. That's a common response; however, your family member may misinterpret your inaction as disagreeing, judging, or worse.
- Don't stay away! Interacting with children with autism is a challenge and you need the right skills. Sometimes love is not enough. Educate yourself as to how children with autism learn differently and how

you can learn the techniques to interact with them based on those methods. Yes, you can use methods you are comfortable with, but if they are not working, don't assume your grandchild is rejecting you; don't assume your grandchild is spoiled or badly behaved. Instead, get involved, learn about autism and your individual loved one, and become part of the team!

- If your adult child/ sister/friend tells you or implies that you are ignoring them and their child, try to determine whether it is true and if it might be because you are unsure of what to do.

- By reading this book you have taken the first step to improving and enhancing your role as a team member.

- Is there a support group for families of children who have autism in your town? Join one! Better still, start one!

- Do you truly accept your loved one's disability? We all want to answer "of course!" Explore the possibility that you might not fully accept some aspects of your loved one's disability. We might not want to view ourselves as being callous, unkind, or unaccepting of differences. But, through no fault of our own, because of what we may have been taught since a very young age, our life experiences and disabilities can sometimes be difficult to accept completely. When this happens, relationships with your child and other family members can be damaged, and resentments, family feuds, and arguments can follow. The first steps toward undoing such damage are to recognize the problem and address your underlying beliefs. Once the process of acceptance starts, you will be liberated from a great burden and allow yourselves to assume your rightful place as true, loving members of the family!

- What if this seems too overwhelming? Consider seeing a counselor who can help you recognize and address underlying beliefs that may be keeping you from fully participating as a loving, supportive family member. This can be a wonderful journey that will benefit you and your loved one with autism. Make an appointment and say, "I am having trouble accepting autism in my grandchild (or niece, nephew, cousin, step-child, or other extended family member). I can't seem to understand what is going on. My family says I am in denial. I am confused but I want to help!" You will not find a more mature, kind, thoughtful, sweet gift to present to your loved ones.

- If you just cannot take that step, then without criticism, give your loved ones space. Let them know you support them and love them, but that you think it would be better to put better boundaries between you, your family member who has autism, and his or her parents. They may have already asked this of you.

- You can still see the other family members, but for now, it's probably best to stay away until you are better able to accept what your loved ones, including the child with autism, are living through and challenged by every day.

Activity C - Create an Autism Survival Kit

1. Water
2. Earplugs or headphones for minimizing expected or unexpected noise
3. Snacks
4. Sunscreen and/or sunglasses
5. Diapers and at least one change of clothing
6. Wet wipes
7. Preferred texture of towels such as soft towels or paper towels
8. Lemon or peppermint-scented lotion to rub under the nose or on the wrist to block overwhelming smells
9. Stickers, small sticky notes, or duct tape to cover toilet and air blower sensors in public restrooms
10. Back-up communication supports such as pictures or paper/pen for print
11. Favorite toys, including those that can be used for repetitive movement when the child is overwhelmed. Be sure to bring power cords!
12. "Chewy toys" that can be used for oral stimulation when needed
13. Dress your loved one in bright colors when going in crowds
14. Include a sticker with your name and contact info on his/her back
15. Have "Autism Information" cards available to give to strangers who may not be accepting. They are available through the Autism Society of America.
16. Teach and practice secret signals or code words your loved one can use if he/she is feeling stressed
17. Tokens or other reinforcers

18. A "first _____, then _____" board with pictures and a pen for drawing/writing what comes first, then next.
19. Visual schedule and/or mini-schedule so the child can predict when activities are likely to be finished
20. Visuals consisting of photos, pic symbols, or pre-printed words so your child can request a break, restroom, or quiet.

Activity D - How to communicate well – for step-parents and everyone else

- Good communication skills are vital and can be learned.
- Use short, specific, clear messages.
- Make and maintain eye contact.
- Don't look away, roll your eyes, frown, or give mixed messages.
- Seek first to understand.
- Listen attentively.
- Don't interrupt.
- Restate what your partner is saying.
- Make sure you understand the issues.
- Take time for each other.
- Take special alone time with your child's sibling.
- Be an effective communicator with schools, doctors.
- Get the most out of each meeting.
- Keep an agenda and write it down.
- Send a letter to schools summarizing any meetings.
- You are a strong member of your loved one's support team.

Activity E - Everyone should practice stress management

- Positively affirm each other's role.
- Acknowledge your own feelings.
- Schedule enjoyable activities, even if only for a short period.
- Practice stress-reduction exercises, such as yoga or simply turning on the radio and dancing!
- Know who to call when stressed and call them.
- Take time for yourself, even if it means you take time for yourself out of the house, while someone watches your child at your home for a while.
- Exercise daily. Exercise may come in fun forms such as jumping on a trampoline or just dancing, even if you do it alone late at night for a few minutes!
- Nurture your spiritual side daily, even if you just take a few seconds.
- Attend a support group and stay connected to the community.

Activity F - Behavior management for extended family members

- Anticipate potential problems and prevent them before they occur.
- Be sure the child has adequate rest before situations in which he or she needs to use good self-control.
- Be sure the child has adequate food intake (including protein) before situations in which he or she needs to use good self-control.
- Attract the child's attention before giving directions!
- Teach and practice what to do and/or say to prevent negative behaviors.
- Present only as much as the child can tolerate.
- Help the child practice correct behavior.
- Avoid waiting for the child to make errors and then correct them. Rather prompt and assist the child to help him or her succeed.
- Practice the necessary skills when everyone is comfortable.
- Catch your loved one being good and praise him or her.
- Remember, if you do not want to be doing something for your loved one when he or she is a young adult, now is the time to teach eating, dressing, toileting, and sleeping through the night independently.
- Identify target outcomes and assess how frequently or how intensively you need to teach your child the necessary skills or behaviors to achieve these outcomes successfully.
- Decide on rewards to be used when desired behaviors are demonstrated.
- Recognize that the strength of the reward needs to balance out the amount of effort it takes for the child to achieve the targeted behavior.

- Review the plan regularly.
- How much progress is the child making toward the target outcomes?
- If there is inadequate improvement, what needs to be done differently?
    - Has treatment been provided for a long enough period?
    - Are the goals realistic?
    - Are you expecting too much too fast?
    - Are the methods of treatment appropriate for the child at this time?
    - Is something else interfering with progress?
    - Does the child need to learn other skills before being able to learn the behavior you have targeted?
- When is it worth intervening?
    - Should you ignore it?
    - Don't make excuses.
- Be consistent about what behavior is acceptable and what is not.
- Remember, "You know more than you think you do."

Activity G - How to handle rude comments in public and even bullying

- Remember, being among people is critical for social success.
- Be prepared by practicing scripted quips and comments to make.
- Carry and pass out autism information cards.
- Keep quips or retorts assertive, not aggressive or angry.
- If anyone offers to help, take them up in it. Be prepared to tell them what they can do to help such as hold the door or make sure that other people let you and the child have some quiet time away from others for a while.
- Provide informational letters in advance for large family functions, so family members understand and can choose to interact with the child more successfully. Those who have not been in this situation do not know what to expect. Knowledge is a powerful coping tool.
- When responding to a bully, avoid any significant aggression. Instead be assertive without being aggressive and do it with an attitude as if you are disgusted or oblivious to their aggression. Do not show fear or anger. Any strong negative emotion will fuel the bully's power.

Activity H - Tips for toileting and eating

A primer on toileting for extended family members

- Always check with parents to ensure that any toileting activity is part of their current plan.
- Any activity related to toileting needs to take place in the bathroom.
- Introduce toileting in play as well. Any toy can go potty!
- Praise your loved one for something before cueing him to do something that is challenging for him.
- Prompt the child to complete the entire toileting routine that includes undressing, sitting on the potty, eliminating, wiping, dressing, flushing, and washing hands. Provide the amount of assistance the child needs to complete this routine successfully, without making mistakes. Physically help the child complete steps to this routine if they are unable to complete the steps correctly on their own.
- Recognize that toileting related tasks consist of numerous small steps and can be more difficult to learn than many people realize. Teach and praise one step at a time.
- Verbally reinforce cooperation even if the child does not eliminate in the toilet.
- Schedule potty breaks *before and after* meals, snacks, bedtime, activities during which the child is running, jumping, swinging, or riding in the car.
- Recognize that positioning on the potty seat is critical to success when learning to eliminate in the toilet. The child needs to be positioned with feet flat on a solid surface and knees even with or higher than the hips.

- Balance difficulties can make sitting challenging. Provide supports as needed, such as seat inserts to prevent "falling in" the toilet bowl and heavy, solid foot stools for proper sitting posture on the toilet and for standing at the sink to wash hands.
- Boys need to be taught to sit for all toileting until they are bowel trained. Having to decide whether to sit or stand adds to the complexity and may interfere with bowel training.
- Make sure the bathroom is not overwhelming with too much light, too much noise, too many people, strong smells (good or bad), or intolerable textures of soap or towels.
- Be patient and gentle.
- Never underestimate your loved one's ability to pick up on your disappointment or disapproval. Remember your child wants nothing more than your approval and praise! Praising cooperation avoids negative behaviors and allows for more effective practice.

Feeding tips for parents include:

- Check with parents to ensure that any feeding activity is part of a current plan.
- Feed the child the way the child should be eating as an adult.
- Eat only in a designated eating area such as the kitchen or dining room, not in the living room while watching TV or in the bedroom. If the family tradition is to snack while in the living room watching TV, then use a specific bowl or other container that is only used for snacking in the living room while watching TV. Rules about eating that apply to the child with autism need to apply to the entire family. If other family members are allowed to dig through the refrigerator for food to grab and eat, then the child with autism will likely learn to do the same without understanding the underlying social rules that

determine when he is allowed to get food out of the refrigerator to eat and when he is not allowed.

- Always have utensils and a napkin available.
- Create a positive atmosphere during meals and snacks.
- Eat at specific times.
- Turn off the television.
- Eat alongside your loved ones as much as possible.
- Introduce novel foods in small portions. Initially, a new food may simply need to be placed on an outer edge of the child's plate on repeated occasions before expecting the child to taste it. Most children need to be able to touch a food before they can tolerate tasting it.
- Make sure the child's seat is comfortable and at the correct height with his feet resting flat on a solid surface. If the child is having to work on sitting up comfortably, he will not be able to direct his focus toward learning behaviors related to eating, such as remaining in his chair, trying new foods, eating foods that are lower preference before eating favorite foods, and tolerating other people talking and sitting near him at the table.
- Don't give up!

Activity I - Adult and Child Rights

Every parent and child has the right to a life of happiness. As a member of your loved one's extended family, you can help ensure that this can happen for them as well.

Check off the rights we all deserve:

❑ I have a right to my opinions.

❑ I have a right to my feelings.

❑ I have a right to make mistakes.

❑ I have a right to come first sometimes.

❑ I have a right to stand up against unfairness.

❑ I have a right to change my mind.

❑ I have a right to say no.

❑ I have a right to be treated with respect.

❑ I have a right to not have to justify my decisions.

❑ I have a right to a love life.

❑ I have a right to find peace within my life.

Resources

Books

Gray, Carol (1994) *Comic Strip Conversations* (Arlington, TX: Future Horizons, Inc.)

Simple drawings illustrating the interactions that comprise the give-and-take of everyday conversations. A useful tool for parents and professionals who work with children with autism and other developmental disorders.

Gray, Carol (2010) *The New Social Story Book Revised and Expanded 10th Anniversary Edition* (Arlington, TX: Future Horizons, Inc.)

Originally fueled by grassroots enthusiasm, and later confirmed as an evidence–based practice, Carol Gray's Social Stories™ have earned the respect of parents and professionals worldwide, while earning the invaluable trust of children and students.

The goal of a Social Story™ is to share accurate information meaningfully and safely, promoting true social understanding. The book provides already–written stories to get you started, plus the direction and tools you'll need to write your own successful Social Story™. May our collective stories inform, guide, and inspire the individuals you care for!

Kranowitz, Carol (2005) *The Out-of Sync Child: Recognizing and Coping with Sensory Processing Disorder, Revised and Updated Edition* (Arlington, TX: Future Horizons, Inc.)

This innovative title broke new ground by identifying Sensory Processing Disorder (SPD), a common but frequently misdiagnosed problem in which the central nervous system misinterprets messages from the senses. This edition features additional information from vision and hearing deficits research, motor skill problems, nutrition and picky eaters, Attention deficit hyperactivity disorder (ADHD), autism, and other related disorders.

You Can Take It With You!

CPSIA information can be obtained
at www.ICGtesting.com
Printed in the USA
JSHW010811160523
41767JS00002B/4